1. Catechism for Adults

CATECHISM
FOR
ADULTS

catechism for adults

(Originally entitled *Introduction to Christian Doctrine*)

by
VERY REVEREND
JAMES ALBERIONE, S.S.P., S.T.D.

NEW VATICAN II EDITION
updated by the Daughters of St. Paul

St. Paul Editions

BX
1961
A6
1971

NIHIL OBSTAT:
    JOHN G. HOGAN

IMPRIMATUR:
    ✠HUMBERTO S. MEDEIROS
        Archbishop of Boston

May 13, 1971

Contents

ORIGIN OF THINGS

The heavens tell the glory of God, and the firmament
proclaims the work of his hands.   *—Psalm 18:1*

The Eternal Father, by a free and hidden plan of His own
wisdom and goodness, created the whole world.... He
created all things out of nothing, pouring into them the
abundance of His wisdom and goodness.
        —Dogmatic Constitution on Church

Did the universe and the things that we see always exist?

Reason and science tell us that the universe and the things that we see did not always exist. They had a beginning. The material universe is not necessary, infinite, perfect; it is contingent, limited, and goes on acquiring new perfections.... Therefore, the universe could not always have existed.

What is the origin of the universe?

If the universe had a beginning, there had to be **Someone** who has always existed (and is therefore eternal), who is necessary, infinite, perfect, independent from all other beings, who brought the universe into existence. This **Someone** we call God.

In what manner did God give origin to the universe?

There are two hypotheses which could be made on the origin of the universe: 1) either it originated through participation of the divine substance; 2) or by creation from nothing.

Can the universe have originated through participation of the divine substance?

It is not possible that the universe had origin through participation of the divine substance or through emanation, as Pantheism and Emanationism teach. **Emanation** means that matter **detached** itself from the divine substance in some manner. But this is repugnant to reason, because the divine substance is spiritual, while the world is material; furthermore the divine substance is most simple and cannot be separated or divided. Therefore it is absurd that the world was originated through emanation from or through participation in the divine substance. It had to receive existence by means of **creation.**

What does "to create" mean?

"To create" means to draw out things from nothing, without making use of any pre-existing substance. To create is proper to God alone.

Can man know the origin of the world?

Reason shows us that the world had origin through creation. But, how this came about remains forever a mystery, notwithstanding the progress of the sciences. To help the weakness of human reason, God Himself has revealed to us, in Sacred Scripture, the origin of the world.

How is the origin of the world as narrated in Genesis to be interpreted?

The Church has always permitted freedom of interpretation in regard to the first chapter of

Genesis. She has defined as a dogma of faith that the world, visible and invisible **was created** by God; she has defined nothing, however, concerning the manner and the time in which it was created and accepts willingly the discoveries of true science. Therefore it is well to follow the conclusions arrived at by the learned, keeping in mind that, to interpret a writing of 1,200 years before Christ, it is necessary to know and hold in due regard the manner of expression and of narration in use at that time.

What does science say in regard to creation?
Positive science holds that creation goes back millions of years; that a great interval of time elapsed between the creation of the world, the appearance and development of life— geological eras—and that man was the last to appear upon earth.

What is the end of creation?
The ultimate end of creation is the glory of God, which He obtains by the manifestation of His perfections: "The entire universe is like a written book," says St. Gregory Nazianzen, "which gives you the material to celebrate the glory of God." The universe is therefore the first "teaching" of God.

GOD THE CREATOR

"In the beginning God created heaven, and earth. And the earth was void and empty, and darkness was upon the face of the deep; and the Spirit of God moved over the waters.

"And God said: Be light made. And light was made. And God saw the light that it was good; and he divided the light from the darkness.... And there was evening and morning, one day.

"And God said: Let there be a firmament made amidst the waters, and let it divide the waters from the waters.... And it was so. And God called the firmament, heaven. And the evening and the morning were the second day.

"God also said: Let the waters that are under the heaven be gathered together into one place, and let the dry land appear. And it was so done. And God called the dry land, earth; and the gathering together of the waters he called seas. And God saw that it was good. And he said: Let the earth bring forth the green herb, and such as may seed, and the fruit tree yielding fruit after its kind, which may have seed in itself upon the earth. And it was so done.... And the evening and the morning were the third day.

"And God said: Let there be lights made in the firmament of heaven, to divide the day and the night, and let them be for signs, and for seasons, and for days and years: to shine in the firmament of heaven, and to give light upon the earth. And it was so done.... And God saw that it was good. And the evening and the morning were the fourth day.

"God also said: Let the waters bring forth the creeping creature having life, and the fowl that may fly over the earth under the firmament of heaven. And God created the great whales, and every living and moving creature.... And

God saw that it was good. And he blessed them, saying: Increase and multiply.... And the evening and morning were the fifth day.

"And God said: Let the earth bring forth the living creature in its kind, cattle and creeping things, and beasts of the earth, according to their kinds. And it was so done. And God saw that it was good" (Genesis 1:1-26).

TRACES OF GOD IN THE UNIVERSE

"Man is not the cause of the world. Anyone who wishes to limit reality, the all, to the thought of man, is playing with the absurd. Our knowledge, our science, our truth does not produce things; it knows them, thinks them, forms images of them, makes them its own spiritually, but it does not create them. Our science, though it is our greatness, is based on great humility. Furthermore, if this cosmos exists, and shows itself to be on the one hand, so traversed by lines of a mysterious order (the sciences tell us so: mathematics, physics especially; the motions, energies, laws... found in it confirm this); and, on the other hand, one would say so charged with a thought not its own, but infused, reflected, operating, and able to be deciphered, known and also used, it is a sign that this cosmos is derived from a transcendent principle, a creative mind, a secret and superior power.... That is: it is created."

—PAUL VI, JULY, 1969

"The more the scientist studies the wonders of the universe, the more he is filled with

admiration and enthusiasm that, in his re-
searches, he discovers and recognizes the
traces of the wisdom of the Creator and
supreme legislator of heaven and earth.''

— PIUS XII

''When I awoke, God the eternal, immense,
omniscient, omnipotent had passed. I saw Him
afar and I remained profoundly astonished. I
followed the traces of His footsteps across the
works of creation and everywhere, even in the
smallest things, what power, what wisdom,
what ineffable perfection!''   — CARL VON LINNEUS

''O Lord, our Lord, how admirable is Your
name in all the earth, You who have exalted
Your majesty above the heavens! (Psalm 8:1).

WHAT IS MAN?

Grant, O Lord, that I may know You, that I may know myself. I want to know God and my soul. Nothing else!
— St. Augustine

What is man? About himself he has expressed, and continues to express, many divergent and even contradictory opinions. In these he often exalts himself as the absolute measure of all things or debases himself to the point of despair. The result is doubt and anxiety. The Church certainly understands these problems. Endowed with light from God, she can offer solutions to them, so that man's true situation can be portrayed and his defects explained, while at the same time his dignity and destiny are justly acknowledged.

— Pastoral Constitution on Church
in Modern World

What is man?
Man is the noblest of visible creatures, composed of a rational soul that is free, simple, spiritual and immortal, and of a material and organic body. Soul and body form one complete being—a person.

What is the soul?
The soul is the spiritual part of man, by which he lives, knows and is free.

Does the human soul really exist?
That the soul of man really exists is proven from the spiritual acts which he performs, such as thinking, reasoning, making decisions, proposing, desiring, etc. Such acts, because they are spiritual, cannot be produced by matter, but by a pure spiritual substance which is called **soul.** We feel that the beginning of such acts is inside of us and not outside, that is, in our very **ego.** This **ego** of ours is always identical with itself: even after many years, in fact, we feel satisfaction or remorse for the past. While the body renews itself continuously, everyone has the intimate certainty of remaining always the same person, with the good and evil he has

done, from childhood to old age. If we were to deny that the soul, that is, the **source or principle** of such spiritual acts as thinking, reasoning, etc., is in us, these acts would be inexplicable.

What is man's origin?

Like the entire universe, man was created by God and is the crown of all His work.

What do science and reason say in regard to the creation of man?

Science tells us nothing positive concerning the first appearance of man upon the earth. There is, however, fairly general agreement among professors of biology and geology that man may have been on earth 800,000 to 1,000,000 years ago.

Reason, considering the marvelous constitution of man, tells us that he cannot have appeared by chance or through blind and slow transformation of beings, as **absolute evolutionism** affirms.

What does Revelation say concerning the creation of man?

As on the creation of the universe, so on the creation of man, Sacred Scripture throws some rays of divine light. It says:

1. that man was created to the image and likeness of God;

2. that he is the noblest of all creatures;

3. that in him there are two principles: one material (the body) and the other spiritual (the soul);

4. that the body was formed from pre-existing matter;

5. that the soul was created immediately from nothing and infused into the body.

In her authentic interpretation of the Sacred Scriptures, what does the Church teach regarding evolution?

"The teaching authority of the Church does not forbid that, in conformity with the present state of human sciences and sacred theology, research and discussions, on the part of men experienced in both fields, take place with regard to the doctrine of evolution, in as far as it inquires into the origin of the human body as coming from pre-existent and living matter—for the Catholic faith obliges us to hold that souls are immediately created by God. However this must be done in such a way that the reasons for both opinions, that is, those favorable and those unfavorable to evolution, be weighed and judged with the necessary seriousness, moderation and measure, and provided that all are prepared to submit to the judgment of the Church, to whom Christ has given the mission of interpreting authentically the Sacred Scriptures and of defending the dogmas of faith. Some however rashly transgress this liberty of discussion, when they act as if the origin of the human body from pre-existing and living matter were already completely certain and proved by the facts which have been discovered up to now and by reasoning on those facts, and as if there were nothing in the sources of divine revelation which demands the greatest moderation and caution in this question."   — PIUS XII, ENCYCLICAL HUMANI GENERIS

Even the theory of "evolutionism" favored today by many scientists and not a few theologians...will not seem acceptable to you where it is not decidedly in accord with the immediate creation of each and every human soul by God, and where it does not regard as decisively important for the fate of mankind the disobedience of Adam, universal protoparent (cf. Council of Trent, session 6, canon 2).

— PAUL VI, ON ORIGINAL SIN, JULY, 1966

From whom does our body receive existence?
Our body receives existence from our parents, by way of natural generation.

From whom does our soul receive existence?
Being spiritual and independent of matter, the soul cannot come from it, nor can it come from the soul of the parents because spirit cannot divide itself. It is directly created by God and infused into the body.

What are the principal faculties of man?
The principal faculties of man are intellect and will. In order to be able to live and act, man is also endowed with internal and external senses.

Is man truly free?
That man is truly free is attested by:
   1. our conscience, which vindicates the

absolute independence of our own actions, both in regard to the forces of nature, as well as in regard to society; we feel that we can do one thing rather than another, or even suspend an action already begun. After the action we feel satisfaction or remorse.

2. It is attested to, besides, by the existence of social laws, which presuppose "individual responsibility"; as also by the unanimous consent of mankind in rewarding good and punishing evil; by the training of children, etc.

3. It is shown us by the development of human institutions and civilizations in which man progresses and develops various ways of living.

4. It is attested to by the possibility which man and society have of progressing.

Is the soul of man truly simple?

The soul of man is simple because it is spiritual. Therefore it is not, like the body, composed of various elements. The soul has neither composition, nor quantity, nor dimensions, nor weight. It is sufficient to reflect on its acts to be convinced of this. The soul, through the intellect, has a clear concept of material and concrete things, as it has of the abstract and the spiritual: for example, from several objects of the same species is formed the universal and abstract concept of the nature of that species; also we have non-material concepts—of beauty, of truth, of love, etc. Our intellect can reflect on itself with perfect

is a celebration
of existence....

U.S. Bishops' Pastoral
Church in Our Day

cognition and re-examine our entire life; we know and enjoy perfect liberty in our spiritual acts, such as reasoning, thinking, loving, etc. All this would be impossible if our soul were composed of parts. Therefore its simplicity appears clearly.

Is the soul of man truly spiritual?

Yes, the soul of man is spiritual. Reason itself tells us this. If the spiritual acts of man, such as understanding and willing, are independent of matter, their **causal-principle,** that is the soul, must also be non-material. This is according to the well-known principle: "As the act is, so is the nature of the cause which produces it."

It is sufficient to consider some of the acts which man performs, to be convinced that they do not come from matter, but from the spirit. We have concepts wholly immaterial and incorporeal, such as: God, virtue, vice, duty, etc. We have desires and resolutions superior to matter: we desire good, truth, honor; we hate vice, dishonesty, injustice.... We have such abstract and universal concepts as: there is no effect without a cause; the whole is greater than a part, etc. We reflect on our acts and, while the body consumes itself with the years and work, the intellect continually perfects itself with age and practice....

All these things affirm in us a **principle** which does not in any way depend for its being on matter and which is entirely **spiritual:** the soul. Therefore **materialism,** the doctrine which does not admit the existence of the spirit, is repugnant to reason.

MAN

"God said: Let us make mankind in our image and likeness; and let them have dominion over the fish of the sea, the birds of the air, the cattle, over all the wild animals and every creature that crawls on the earth. And God created man in his image.... Male and female he created them. Then God blessed them, saying: 'Be fruitful and multiply; fill the earth and subdue it'" (Genesis 1:26-28).

"O Lord, what is man, that you should be mindful of him?...

"You have made him little less than the angels, and crowned him with glory and honor.

"You have given him rule over the works of your hands..." (Psalm 8:5-9).

"Man is composed of entirely different parts. He is celestial on the one hand and terrestrial on the other. He is an angel, an animal, a miracle, a center, a world, a god, a nothing surrounded by God, in need of God, capable of possessing God and full of God if he wants."

— PIERRE DE BERULLE

"Though made of body and soul, man is one. Through his bodily composition he gathers to himself the elements of the material world; thus they reach their crown through him, and through him raise their voice in free praise of the Creator. For this reason man is not allowed to despise his bodily life; rather he is obliged to regard his body as good and honorable since God has created it and will raise it up on the last day. Nevertheless, wounded by sin, man experiences rebellious stirrings in his body. But the very dignity of man postulates that man glorify God in his body and forbid it to serve the evil inclinations of his heart.

"Now, man is not wrong when he regards himself as superior to bodily concerns, and as more than a speck of nature or a nameless constituent of the city of man. For by his interior qualities he outstrips the whole sum of mere things. He plunges into the depths of reality whenever he enters into his own heart; God, who probes the heart, awaits him there; there he discerns his proper destiny beneath the eyes of God. Thus, when he recognizes in himself a spiritual and immortal soul, he is not being mocked by a fantasy born only of physical or social influences, but is rather laying hold of the proper truth of the matter."

—PASTORAL CONSTITUTION ON CHURCH IN MODERN WORLD

MAN'S LOFTY DESTINY

One is the community of all peoples, one their origin, for God made the whole human race to live over the face of the earth. One also is their final goal, God. His providence, His manifestations of goodness, His saving design extend to all men, until that time when the elect will be united in the Holy City, the city ablaze with the glory of God, where the nations will walk in His light.

Men expect from the various religions answers to the unsolved riddles of the human condition, which today, even as in former times, deeply stir the hearts of men: What is man? What is the meaning, the aim of our life? What is moral good, what sin? Whence suffering and what purpose does it serve? Which is the road to true happiness? What are death, judgment and retribution after death? What, finally, is that ultimate inexpressible mystery which encompasses our existence: whence do we come, and where are we going?

—Declaration on Relation of Church to Non-Christian Religions

Is the soul of man truly immortal?

That the soul of man is truly immortal is a truth constantly admitted by the whole human race and by our own conscience. In fact: 1) Goodness, justice and wisdom require the good to be rewarded and the evil to be punished. This does not always take place in the present life. A second life is therefore necessary. 2) The soul is, of its own nature, simple and spiritual; hence it cannot break up into parts or depend upon matter, or perish. 3) Human instinct invincibly desires a full and unending life with intuition of the infinite. We know that, to every natural instinct, there corresponds a law of nature. Therefore, the soul of man **is** immortal. 4) This certainty has been held in all times and by all religions and civilizations; the most learned men, the best philosophers and thinkers of all ages have constantly professed such a doctrine. Thus, the great souls, the great benefactors of humanity, the lovers of justice and of goodness have believed in man's immortality.

If the soul is immortal, what follows?

The soul being immortal, man must order his whole present life to the future, so as to win immortal bliss.

What, therefore, is the present life?

The present life is the time God grants to every man to prepare himself for his eternal happiness.

Who, then, are the truly wise?

The truly wise are only and always those who in the present life consider, direct and do everything in view of the future life, since this depends on the present life.

Does human life have a purpose?

Yes, human life has a purpose. God, the most wise Being, could not have made the most noble of His earthly creatures without an aim. On the other hand, the dignity of the human person requires it: an intelligent being cannot act blindly, without a worthy goal.

What is man's ultimate end?

The ultimate end of man is natural happiness without end, because only this can fully satisfy every human desire. God willed, nevertheless, with His omnipotence, to elevate man to an end superior to his nature.

Is supreme happiness possible?

Supreme happiness is possible, because it is absurd to think that God should have destined man to an unattainable end. Man would be unhappy if he could not obtain that which forms his natural and supreme tendency.

Can material goods constitute man's happiness?
External and earthly goods such as riches, pleasure, power, etc., cannot constitute the happiness of man, being goods inferior to his dignity, external, passing and possessed only by a few persons. Such goods are **means** to attain perfect happiness, but they are **not** perfect happiness.

And can internal goods form the happiness of man?
Not even internal goods, such as wisdom, virtue, family joys, friendship, etc., can form the happiness of man, because even these are not unmixed with sorrows and are not eternal.

Therefore, what will be the object of our supreme happiness?
The object of our supreme happiness is God alone, because He alone is the eternal good. He alone can satisfy fully and perpetually our intellect, desires, aspirations and all the spiritual and corporal faculties of man.

With what means can man arrive at happiness upon earth?
Man can arrive at **natural** happiness upon the earth: 1) by knowing God; 2) by observing the natural law; 3) by respecting God and neighbor according to human reason.

Can man attain complete happiness upon the earth?
Complete happiness cannot be attained in this life, where the evils are many, the good things few and always passing; but rather in

the next life, where the whole man will be fully satisfied in God: satisfied in his intellect, because God is supreme and infinite truth; satisfied in his will, because God is perfect and essential goodness; satisfied in his sentiment, because God is beauty, peace, happiness itself.

Therefore, what is the value of the present life?

The value of the present life is almost nothing if considered in itself, because of the many evils and the few and insufficient goods. Instead, it is an inestimable good considered as the prelude to eternity, since eternal happiness or unhappiness depends on it.

Does this mean that man should neglect earthly progress?

"Throughout the course of the centuries, men have labored to better the circumstances of their lives through a monumental amount of individual and collective effort. To believers, this point is settled: considered in itself, this human activity accords with God's will. For man, created to God's image, received a mandate to subject to himself the earth and all it contains, and to govern the world with justice and holiness; a mandate to relate himself and the totality of things to Him who was to be acknowledged as the Lord and Creator of all. Thus, by the subjection of all things to man, the name of God would be wonderful in all the earth."

—PASTORAL CONSTITUTION ON CHURCH IN MODERN WORLD

What awaits man after death?

"Since we know not the day nor the hour, on our Lord's advice we must be constantly vigilant so that having finished the course of our earthly life, we may merit to enter into the marriage feast with Him and to be numbered among the blessed (cf. Matthew 25:31-46) and may not be ordered to go into eternal fire (cf. Matthew 25:41) like the wicked and slothful servant (cf. Matthew 25:26), into the exterior darkness where 'there will be the weeping and the gnashing of teeth' (Matthew 22:13). For before we reign with Christ in glory, all of us will be made manifest 'before the tribunal of Christ, so that each one may receive what he has won through the body, according to his works, whether good or evil' (2 Corinthians 5:10) and at the end of the world 'they who have done good shall come forth unto resurrection of life; but those who have done evil unto resurrection of judgment' (John 5:29)."

— DOGMATIC CONSTITUTION ON CHURCH

What are the evils of sin?

"Every sin causes a perturbation in the universal order established by God in His ineffable wisdom and infinite charity, and the destruction of immense values with respect to the sinner himself and to the human community. Christians throughout history have always regarded sin not only as a transgression of divine law but also—though not always in a direct and evident way—as contempt for or disregard of the friendship between God and man, just as they have regarded it as a real and unfathomable offense against God and indeed an ungrateful rejection of the love of God shown us through Jesus Christ, who called His disciples friends and not servants."

—APOSTOLIC CONSTITUTION ON INDULGENCES

Is there a place of purification beyond the grave?

"It is a divinely revealed truth that sins bring punishments inflicted by God's sanctity and justice. These must be expiated either on this earth through the sorrows, miseries and calamities of this life and above all through death, or else in the life beyond through fire and torments or 'purifying' punishments. Therefore it has always been the conviction of the faithful that the paths of evil are fraught with many stumbling blocks and bring adversities, bitterness and harm to those who follow them.

"These punishments are imposed by the just and merciful judgment of God for the purification of souls, the defense of the sanctity of the moral order and the restoration of the glory of God to its full majesty....

"In purgatory, the souls of those who died in the charity of God and truly repentant, but before satisfying with worthy fruits of penance for sins committed and for omissions are cleansed after death with purgatorial punishments."

—APOSTOLIC CONSTITUTION ON INDULGENCES

CHOOSING OUR FUTURE

"In the depths of his conscience, man detects a law which he does not impose upon himself, but which holds him to obedience. Always summoning him to love good and avoid evil, the voice of conscience when necessary speaks to his heart: do this, shun that. For man has in his heart a law written by God; to obey it is the very dignity of man; according to it he will be judged. Conscience is the most secret core and sanctuary of a man. There he is alone with God, whose voice echoes in his depths. In a wonderful manner conscience reveals that law which is fulfilled by love of God and neighbor.

"In fidelity to conscience, Christians are joined with the rest of men in the search for truth, and for the genuine solution to the numerous problems which arise in the life of individuals from social relationships. Hence the more right conscience holds sway, the more persons and groups turn aside from blind choice and strive to be guided by the objective norms of morality.

"Conscience frequently errs from invincible ignorance without losing its dignity. The same cannot be said for a man who cares but little for truth and goodness, or for a conscience which by degrees grows practically sightless as a result of habitual sin.

"Only in freedom can man direct himself toward goodness. Our contemporaries make much of this freedom and pursue it eagerly; and rightly to be sure. Often however they

foster it perversely as a license for doing whatever pleases them, even if it is evil. For its part,
authentic freedom is an exceptional sign of
the divine image within man. For God has willed
that man remain 'under the control of his own
decisions,' so that he can seek his Creator
spontaneously, and come freely to utter and
blissful perfection through loyalty to Him.
Hence man's dignity demands that he act
according to a knowing and free choice that is
personally motivated and prompted from within,
not under blind internal impulse nor by mere
external pressure.

"Man achieves such dignity when, emanci-
pating himself from all captivity to passion,
he pursues his goal in a spontaneous choice of
what is good, and procures for himself through
effective and skillful action, apt helps to that
end. Since man's freedom has been damaged
by sin, only by the aid of God's grace can he
bring such a relationship with God into full
flower. Before the judgment seat of God each
man must render an account of his own life,
whether he has done good or evil."

— PASTORAL CONSTITUTION ON CHURCH IN MODERN WORLD

THIRST FOR GOD

"Without God, our eagerness for life becomes
anxious and our plans for the future lead to
inevitable futility. If there is no God at the
beginning and at the end of life, then man
lives with little meaning. He is born by accident
and is destined for extinction. One day his
history and his world will vanish without a trace

that he was here. Without God all the human family will one day perish without ever having known why they were here, for what they were made, to what purpose they had lived so glorious and tragic a history. Without God, human life tends to dust, fatally and forever.

"Christians cannot accept this gospel of despair. They ask man, heroic in the dreams he has achieved, to dare dream of collaboration with God. They invite our courageous century to attain the further courage of faith. They invite a waiting, expectant age, in all its waiting, to await even God."

— U.S. BISHOPS' PASTORAL, CHURCH IN OUR DAY

"One would almost say that the days of my existence are counted and that it hurries to regain time uselessly lost, by occupying every minute of the day.... To work here on earth, to rest for all eternity in the bosom of God, to saturate with divine love the soul which has found its goal! When will I seize this goal? Work hastens the days, renders the days moments for me and the years hours—to run more rapidly to where I feel myself called. Why such hurry, such eagerness to run, to accumulate, to work? To run sooner to the Lord and never more detach myself from Him."

— RINO ROSSI

"Every man, through natural inclination, desires to know. But of what use is knowledge without the fear of God? Certainly the humble peasant, who serves God, is better than the proud learned man, who contemplates the path of the stars and neglects his own salvation. The most high and useful lesson is this: **to really know oneself.**

"O my God, Who are Truth itself, unite me to You with eternal love. Let the learned hold their peace; let all creatures be silent in Your sight; speak to me, You alone!"

— IMITATION OF CHRIST

A PERSONAL, PROVIDENT GOD

Oh, the depth of the riches of the wisdom and of the knowledge of God! How incomprehensible are his judgments and unsearchable his ways! Who has known the mind of the Lord, or who has been his counselor? Or who has first given to him, that recompense should be made him? For from him and through him and unto him are all things. To him be the glory forever. Amen.

— Romans 9:33-36

God is — and more, He is real. He lives, a personal, provident God, infinitely good; and not only good in Himself, but also immeasurably good to us.

— COUNCIL CLOSING SPEECHES

41

Who is God?

God is the heavenly Father who created us, the Supreme Being, all-perfect and infinite. All that which can be said of God, regarding His existence, is contained in this: that He is the necessary Being and the Beginning of all things. In Him essence and existence are identical. From this concept of **necessary Being** stem the infinite perfections of God.

Are you certain of the existence of God?

I am certain of the existence of God for the following reasons:

1) Because the universe **exists** without having in itself the necessary reasons for its existence.

2) Because this universe is **ordered** according to uniform, constant, harmonious cosmic laws arranged in an hierarchical manner, and this requires intelligence.

3) Because **movement** animates the entire universe and **life** circulates without rest in the most admirable variety of beings, an impossible thing without its depending on a superior life.

4) Other proofs of the existence of God are: the **universal consensus** of peoples; **the necessity of a moral law** which supposes a Supreme Legislator, and above all, for each individual, that **sense of duty** (conscience) and that **innate desire for an absolute happiness** which cannot be attained in this life.

Do the things we see really exist?
Yes, the things we see really exist: 1) this fact is attested to us by our senses through which we see, feel, hear, taste...; 2) it is assured us by our awareness that we exist; 3) it is confirmed by reason and the universal consensus of mankind. Do we not explain effects by their respective causes? Therefore, **Idealism**—the philosophical doctrine which makes the reality of things depend on our ideas—is repugnant to reason, to experience and to the consensus of peoples.

If God exists, what is to be said of atheism?
Atheism—the doctrine which denies the existence of God—is contrary to right reason, to the universal consensus of men and to our very conscience.

Is atheism possible?
Yes, it is possible for men to live **practically** as though there did not exist either God or the distinction between good and evil, or future reward or punishment. The pressure of the concrete problems of life, the impetus of the passions, an indifferent family environment and a secular education can, for a certain

period of life, divert the interest of man from the problem of God.

Can a convinced atheist be found?

In the present condition of humanity, because of the materialistic doctrines which are so persistently taught, it is possible to find **theoretical atheists.** The man who reasons seriously, however, will always have at least a confused persuasion of the existence of God. First of all the great phenomena of nature, then the decisive facts of human existence such as birth and death, and the most trying problem, that is, the suffering of the just man upon this earth and the frequent fortune of the evil man—all this, sooner or later, must impose on the human mind the problem of God.

Could a godless society better foster human development?

"True, man can organize the world apart from God, but without God man can organize it in the end only to man's detriment. An isolated humanism is an inhuman humanism. There is no true humanism but that which is open to the Absolute and is conscious of a vocation which gives human life its true meaning. Far from being the ultimate measure of all things, man can only realize himself by reaching beyond himself. As Pascal has said so well: 'Man infinitely surpasses man.'"

—PAUL VI, ENCYCLICAL, DEVELOPMENT OF PEOPLES

Does only one God exist or several gods?

Only one God exists, because being the first Principle and the first Cause of all things, infinitely perfect, He can be but one. If there were several gods, no one would be infinite, each one lacking the perfection of the others. The existence of several gods, equally supreme and infinite, is repugnant to reason.

Is God a personal being or are He and nature one and the same?

God and nature are not one and the same, because God has all attributes in an infinite degree and is changeless, whereas nature has no such perfection.

What are the perfections of God?

The perfections or divine attributes are unity, simplicity, immutability, eternity, omnipresence, omniscience, sanctity, justice, goodness, wisdom, beauty—attributes which form a sole oneness, indistinct and inseparable from the divine essence.

Is God most perfect?

God is most perfect because He has all the perfections in an infinite degree. He is perfection itself.

How do you show that God is most perfect?

That God is most perfect results from this:
1) That He is the author of the perfections which are found in creatures, such as goodness, wisdom, life, beauty, personality, activity, etc.
2) If God were to lack any perfection, He would have only a **share** of existence. Instead, God is Existence itself. Therefore He possesses, in its highest form, every perfection that exists.

Is God provident?

Yes, God is provident. He has assigned an end to all creatures and being goodness itself, He is well disposed toward them and toward their end: therefore, He necessarily provides them with the means to attain it. God can do this directly, but often He makes use of creatures themselves whom He makes participants in the execution of His providential plan. The means of which God makes use to lead us to our end (joy and sorrow, long or short life, etc.) are often unknown to us. This is why, most of the time, the wise work of Divine Providence remains for us wrapped in obscurity. Man, by abusing his liberty, can render useless, in his own regard, the work of Divine Providence.

Can we truly say that God cares for each one of us?

We may affirm with Cardinal Newman: "What a joy and consolation it is to feel that God beholds me and calls me by name; that He knows all that is in me—all my peculiar feelings and thoughts, my strength and my weakness.... I do not love myself more than He loves me. I cannot shrink from pain more than He dislikes my bearing it; if He puts it on me, it is as I would put it on myself, if I am wise, for a great reward here and hereafter. I am not only His creature, but one redeemed and sanctified—His adopted child. I am one of those for whom Christ offered up His last prayer and sealed it with His precious blood."

What is God's providential order regarding creatures?

God's providential order is as follows: 1) all the inferior beings—mineral, vegetable, animal—serve man; 2) man must glorify God and he glorifies Him by aspiring to his eternal happiness: he who saves himself gives the maximum glory to God.

Why then, are there so many social inequalities?

This depends in part on the nature of the individual (not all have the same talents); in part on human will and liberty, because of which not all employ the same industriousness and the same care for their own progress and betterment, and respect for justice and charity. Besides, good and evil do not always have remuneration in this life; remuneration will be complete and eternal only in the next life.

If God is all-perfect, what practical consequences derive from this?

The better a man lives according to God, the more perfect he will be.

Does God have dominion over man?

As Creator and Lord, God has a right to total dominion over man and, in the first place, over his mind. Since God is infinite Truth and perfectly veracious, man must believe His words when He speaks, because He can neither deceive nor be deceived.

Is man obliged to seek the truth?

Man is obliged to seek the truth, and, among the various religions, embrace that which is proved to be true. Whoever reasons, feels this duty.

Are faith and knowledge the same thing?

No. Knowledge is the cognition of things by means of **reason** and is the first step towards faith. Faith is the apprehension of truths by means of **revelation**. The virtue of faith is a divine gift and is exercised with acts of the intelligence under the influence of free will and the grace of God.

Can the truths known by the light of reason be objects of faith?

The natural truths, which at the same time are revealed by God, can be objects of faith, if they are professed by relying on the authority of God the revealer. The same truth—for example, the knowledge of God—can be obtained from two sources, of which one is human and the other divine. The divine source, however, is by far superior to the human one, rendering the supernatural knowledge of God richer, more perfect, more certain.

Is faith an escape?

"Our faith in God is not an escape from life, a reprieve from responsibility, or a hope with no foundation. Our faith in God is a celebration of existence, an affirmation of indestructible meaning in every man and in man's world, a refusal to live with the fiction that human inventions or even human life can offer all the answers and all the healing man needs. A man who cannot aspire beyond the boundaries of space and the limits of time is of all creatures the most pathetic."

— U. S. BISHOPS' PASTORAL, CHURCH IN OUR DAY

Is faith especially necessary in our day?

"Today it is necessary to have a vital and dynamic faith, able to overcome those difficulties that we encounter today.

"For this reason I believe we will have to struggle within the Church itself—and it will not always be an easy task—to keep the place we wish to give to God in our personal life and in the life of society, having the courage to take a stand when these fundamental attitudes are wrongly attacked."

— JEAN CARDINAL DANIELOU, CHRISTIAN FAITH AND TODAY'S MAN

THE TRIUNE GOD

"We believe in one only God, Father, Son and Holy Spirit, creator of things visible such as this world in which our transient life passes, of things invisible such as the pure spirits which are also called angels, and creator in each man of his spiritual and immortal soul.

"We believe that this only God is absolutely one in His infinitely holy essence as also in all His perfections, in His omnipotence, His infinite knowledge, His providence, His will and His love. He is **He who is,** as He revealed to Moses; and He is **love,** as the apostle John teaches us: so that these two names, being and love, express ineffably the same divine reality of Him who has wished to make Himself known to us, and who, 'dwelling in light inaccessible,' is in Himself above every name, above every thing and above every created intellect. God alone can give us right and full knowledge of this reality by revealing Himself as Father, Son and Holy Spirit, in whose eternal life we are by grace called to share, here below in the obscurity of faith and after death in eternal light. The mutual bonds which eternally constitute the Three Persons, who are each one and the same divine being, are the blessed inmost life of God thrice holy, infinitely beyond all that we can conceive in human measure. We give thanks, however, to the divine goodness that very many believers can testify with us before men to the unity of God, even though they know not the mystery of the most holy Trinity."

—PAUL VI, CREDO OF THE PEOPLE OF GOD

THE GODLESS

"The word atheism is applied to phenomena which are quite distinct from one another. For while God is expressly denied by some, others believe that man can assert absolutely nothing about Him. Still others use such a method to scrutinize the question of God as to make it seem devoid of meaning.

"Many, unduly transgressing the limits of the positive sciences, contend that everything can be explained by this kind of scientific reasoning alone, or by contrast, they altogether disallow that there is any absolute truth.

"Some laud man so extravagantly that their faith in God lapses into a kind of anemia, though they seem more inclined to affirm man than to deny God.

"Again some form for themselves such a fallacious idea of God that when they repudiate this figment they are by no means rejecting the God of the Gospel.

"Some never get to the point of raising questions about God, since they seem to experience no religious stirrings nor do they see why they should trouble themselves about religion.

"Moreover, atheism results not rarely from a violent protest against the evil in this world, or from the absolute character with which certain human values are unduly vested, and which thereby already accords them the stature of God.

"Modern civilization itself often complicates the approach to God not for any essential reason but because it is so heavily engrossed in earthly affairs.

"Undeniably, those who willfully shut out God from their hearts and try to dodge religious questions are not following the dictates of their consciences, and hence are not free of blame; yet believers themselves frequently bear some responsibility for this situation. For, taken as a whole, atheism is not a spontaneous development but stems from a variety of causes, including a critical reaction against religious beliefs, and in some places against the Christian religion in particular.

"Hence believers can have more than a little to do with the birth of atheism. To the extent that they neglect their own training in the faith, or teach erroneous doctrine, or are deficient in their religious, moral or social life, they must be said to conceal rather than reveal the authentic face of God and religion."

—PASTORAL CONSTITUTION ON CHURCH IN MODERN WORLD

MAN NEEDS GOD

"You say: 'We do not need God!' And in your spirit remorse sits darkly, and the sorrowful desolation of your skepticism desires the embrace of the divine Consoler!...

"You do not need God...and why so much discouragement, why this indefinable thirst for a hidden and remote good?... We do not need God! And God needs you...because the father needs the affection of his children and the Creator has His delights in creatures. He has need of you whom sophism had led astray, of you whom vice has perverted, of you who are without faith and comfort, to uplift your heart to the joy of His ineffable consolations!

"...Oh, do not fear that His yoke is harsh: do not fear that He will refuse you after your refusal, that He will abandon you after your abandonment, that He will insult you after your blasphemy and mock at your desperation! No. He is a father. Run to His paternal and divine embrace, inebriate yourselves in the sweetness of the paternal home, in the peace of His consolations!"   —CONTARDO FERRINI

"Of all the forces which humanity possesses, faith is certainly the greatest, and it is with

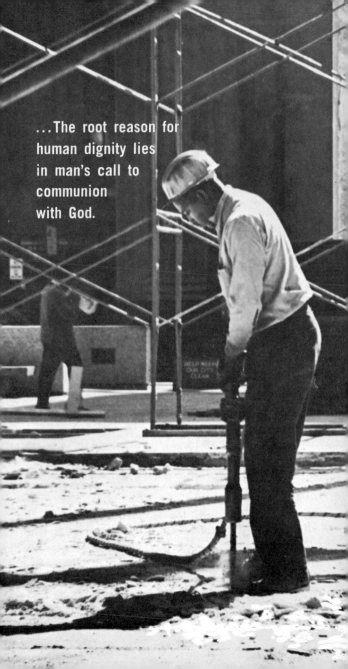

...The root reason for
human dignity lies
in man's call to
communion
with God.

full reason that the Holy Gospel attributes to it the force to move mountains. To give man faith is to multiply his powers. The great events of history have been brought about by believing men, who had nothing but faith for their law."

—LE BON

"In praying, do not multiply words...; for your Father knows what you need before you ask him. In this manner therefore shall you pray: **Our Father** who art in heaven, hallowed be thy name. Thy kingdom come, thy will be done on earth, as it is in heaven. Give us this day our daily bread. And forgive us our debts, as we also forgive our debtors. And lead us not into temptation, but deliver us from evil. Amen" (Matthew 6:7-13).

RESPONSE TO THE CREATOR'S LOVE

In the face of the modern development of the world, the number constantly swells of the people who raise the most basic questions or recognize them with a new sharpness: what is man? What is this sense of sorrow, of evil, of death, which continues to exist despite so much progress? What purpose have these victories purchased at so high a cost? What can man offer to society, what can he expect from it? What follows this earthly life?

...The root reason for human dignity lies in man's call to communion with God. From the circumstances of his origin man is already invited to converse with God. For man would not exist were he not created by God's love and constantly preserved by it; and he cannot live fully according to truth unless he freely acknowledges that love and devotes himself to his Creator.

—Pastoral Constitution on Church in Modern World

It is easier to find a city without walls, houses, laws, money, than a people without a God, without prayer, without religious rites, without sacrifices. *—Plutarch*

What bonds unite man to God?

Man is united to God by bonds of subjection, adoration and love, God being the principle and giver of every good, our provident Lord, ultimate end of the universe and of man. From this arises the obligation of religion.

What is meant by religion?

Religion is that totality of truths to believe, of moral principles to observe and of acts of worship to render to God, with which we honor God Himself and order all our life to Him.

Can all religions be true?

It is impossible for all religions to be true, because truth, like holiness, is **one.** The various religions, instead, often contradict themselves in doctrine, in principles of morals and in worship. However, there are **elements** of truth and holiness in the various religions, since the Spirit of God is at work in the world.

Of what use is religion?

Religion serves to place and keep man in the necessary vital relationship with God, both for the needs of earthly life, as well as, and above all, for eternal beatitude.

Why is religion necessary for the future life?
Religion is necessary for the future life, because God is the just remunerator of the good and evil done during one's earthly life.

How many kinds of religion are there?
Religion can be **natural** and **supernatural**. **Natural** religion would be the body of truths, of religious duties and acts of worship conformable to human reason. **Supernatural** religion is the body of truths, of duties and of acts of worship conformable to divine Revelation. The former guides us to the knowledge, to the service and to the natural worship of God. The latter leads us to the supernatural end by making use of supernatural means which are truths of faith, Christian morals, the sacrifice of the Mass, the sacraments and prayer.

Natural religion is imperfect in many respects. Ignorance, passion and ceaseless activity make it difficult for man's intellect to grasp and reflect upon all the truths and moral teachings that should be within the reach of his reason. Strength of passion and weakness of will make it morally impossible for man (unaided) always to do good and avoid evil. Man needs the constant inward light and strength that supernatural religion affords.

In what manner does man exercise the virtue of religion?
Man exercises the virtue of religion by ordering his life to the **knowledge,** to the **service** and to the **love** of God by means of due worship.

Can man know God?
Man cannot know God directly, but he can know Him and demonstrate with certainty His existence by means of the things which exist.

What are the means of knowing God?
The means of knowing God are principally three: 1) reflection and religious instruction; 2) prayer; 3) right intention.

How is God loved?
God is loved by considering Him as the Supreme Good and by desiring Him as our eternal happiness. If genuine, this love expresses itself in deeds of service to God and to neighbor. "How can he who does not love his brother, whom he sees, love God, whom he does not see?" (1 John 4:20)

How is God served?
God is served by observing the ten commandments, the written expression of the natural law, and by serving our fellow man. Thus, we worship our Creator and foster the spiritual and temporal welfare of mankind.

Must the whole human being serve God?
Yes, the soul as well as the body must serve God; the body, however, serves God by obeying the soul.

With what acts of worship is God honored?
God is honored with internal, external and public acts of worship. In particular we honor Him by dedicating to Him a part of our time, by respecting His name, our vows and oaths.

What must our internal and external acts of worship express?

Since God is the Supreme Majesty, our acts of worship, both internal and external, must above all express adoration, then gratitude for benefits received, reparation for evil committed, and supplication for one's own needs.

Why must worship also be external?

Worship and religion are to be shown also externally because the whole of man, both soul and body, depends on God, and external manifestation is spontaneous in him who has internal religious conviction. The external manifestation strengthens the internal spirit and is of good example in society. Man naturally forms part of **society** which, as such, has its collective duties toward God.

Must society, as such, also show itself religious?

Yes, society, too, must show itself religious, because it also has its origin from God and is composed of human beings. Furthermore, religion is of great advantage to society. Hence society itself must publicly profess and promote religion and give to individuals the possibility of fulfilling their religious duties.

Does man also have duties toward himself?

Yes, man also has duties toward himself: some concern the soul, others the body. In particular he has the duty of self-preservation and of striving towards a plane of life that is ever more elevated—intellectually, morally and materially.

Which is the most noble part of man?
The most noble part of man is the soul, because it is spiritual and immortal. It must direct the body, too, to its ultimate end, in a reasonable manner.

Will the body also be rewarded or punished in the future life?
Yes, certainly, because God is just. In doing good or evil the soul and body work together. Therefore....

RELIGION

"I respect religion and feel the power it has over the human soul. The concept of the divinity, of the superior order, of a future life ... is the balm of every suffering soul, transfixed and tried every day by fatigue and misfortune. And woe to us if we should go against it! As Minister of Italy, I feel it a duty to educate our youth in the great principles, among which the **religious principles** are the first."
— GUY BACCELLI

"Religion is the bond of universal brotherhood, the impulse of operative love, the educator of strong men."
— NICHOLAS TOMMASEO

"God gave me an intelligence, but this must not be displayed except to know Him; God has given me a will, but this must not and cannot have any other role than to take pleasure in His perfections; God has given me strength of spirit and of body, but these must not be used except to serve Him and to contribute to His glory."
— JOSEPH TONIOLO

"The highest norm of human life is the divine law—eternal, objective and universal—whereby God orders, directs and governs the entire universe and all the ways of the human community by a plan conceived in wisdom and love. Man has been made by God to participate in this law, with the result that, under the gentle disposition of divine Providence, he can come to perceive ever more fully the truth that is unchanging.

"Wherefore every man has the duty, and therefore the right, to seek the truth in matters religious in order that he may with prudence form for himself right and true judgments of conscience, under use of all suitable means.

"Truth, however, is to be sought after in a manner proper to the dignity of the human person and his social nature. The inquiry is to be free, carried on with the aid of teaching or instruction, communication and dialogue, in the course of which men explain to one another the truth they have discovered, or think they have discovered, in order thus to assist one another in the quest for truth.

"Moreover, as the truth is discovered, it is by a personal assent that men are to adhere to it.

"On his part, man perceives and acknowledges the imperatives of the divine law through the mediation of conscience. In all his activity a man is bound to follow his conscience in order that he may come to God, the end and purpose of life. It follows that he is not to be forced to act in a manner contrary to his conscience. Nor, on the other hand, is he to be restrained from acting in accordance with his conscience, especially in matters religious. The reason is that the exercise of religion, of its very nature, consists before all else in those internal, voluntary and free acts whereby man sets the course of his life directly toward God. No merely human power can either command or prohibit acts of this kind.

"The social nature of man, however, itself requires that he should give external expression to his internal acts of religion: that he should share with others in matters religious; that he should profess his religion in community. Injury therefore is done to the human person and to the very order established by God for human life, if the free exercise of religion is denied in society, provided just public order is observed."   — DECLARATION ON RELIGIOUS FREEDOM

EVER IN GOD'S CARE

God, who through the Word creates all things and keeps them in existence, gives men an enduring witness to Himself in created realities. Planning to make known the way of heavenly salvation, He went further and from the start manifested Himself to our first parents. Then after their fall His promise of Redemption aroused in them the hope of being saved and from that time on He ceaselessly kept the human race in His care, to give eternal life to those who perseveringly do good in search of salvation.
—Dogmatic Constitution on Divine Revelation

The command of the Lord is firm, instructing the ignorant.
—Psalm 18:8

How is the religious history of humanity divided?
The religious history of humanity is divided into six parts:

1) Creation of Adam and Eve and their elevation to the supernatural state;

2) the fall of Adam and Eve and the punishment inflicted by God upon them and upon their descendants;

3) expectation of and preparation for the coming of the Redeeming Messiah;

4) Incarnation of the Son of God and His redemptive work;

5) institution and life of the Church, which applies the fruits of the redemption to men of all times and of all places;

6) consummation of the ages with the end of the world, resurrection of all mankind and the last judgment.

Is the creation of man the work of God, One and Triune?
Yes, the creation of man is the work of God, One and Triune. Man is one in nature and endowed with intelligence, will and sentiment; he is made to the image and likeness of God.

Was Adam created alone?

Adam was not created alone; God gave him a companion, of whom the Holy Bible says that she was made from a part of his body. She was the first woman and from their union came the entire human family.

What is meant by "elevation to the supernatural state"?

By "elevation to the supernatural state" is meant that besides having endowed Adam and Eve with a body and a soul, God infused in them, solely out of goodness, the gift of His holy grace, and assigned to man a supernatural end so that he could one day participate in His eternal beatitude.

Besides grace, what other gifts did man receive from God?

Besides having received grace, Adam and Eve were created immune from concupiscence, from ignorance, from pain and from the necessity of dying.

Did God put our first parents to a trial?

Yes. In order that they might know the complete dominion of their Creator, God put our first parents to a trial of submission and of obedience. On obedience depended the conservation of grace; rebellion, on the other hand, meant the loss, for them and for their descendants, of those gifts with which He had freely enriched them.

Were Adam and Eve obedient to God?

On the pretext of elevating their personal

condition, our first parents dared to rebel against God. Then, for their fault and in accord with the divine warning, they were stripped—they and their descendants—of divine grace; they were subjected to the passions, to death, to pain and to concupiscence. Thus, they exposed us all to the danger of eternal damnation.

In what does original sin consist?

Original sin consists in the privation of original grace, that is, of supernatural life, which according to divine disposition we should have, but do not because the head of humanity, with his disobedience, deprived himself and all his descendants of it. God does not punish with the torments of hell those who die with only original sin, but without grace no one can enter into paradise.

"We believe that in Adam all have sinned, which means that the original offense committed by him caused human nature, common to all men, to fall to a state in which it bears the consequences of that offense, and which is not the state in which it was at first in our first parents—established as they were in holiness and justice, and in which man knew neither evil nor death. It is human nature so fallen, stripped of the grace that clothed it, injured in its own natural powers and subjected to the dominion of death, that is transmitted to all men, and it is in this sense that every man is born in sin."

—PAUL VI, CREDO OF THE PEOPLE OF GOD

How must Scripture be understood with regard to the doctrine of original sin?

Pope Paul, in addressing biblical scholars, gives a clear answer:

"Convinced that the doctrine of original sin regarding both its existence and universality, its character as true sin even in the descendants of Adam and its sad consequences for soul and body, is a truth revealed by God in various passages of the Old and of the New Testament, but especially in the texts you well know of Genesis 3:1-20, and of the Letter to the Romans 5:12-19, always take care, in scrutinizing and specifying the meaning of biblical texts, to observe the indispensable norms which stem from the analogy of faith, from the declarations and definitions of the councils and from the documents issued by the Apostolic See. Thus you will be certain of respecting 'what the Catholic Church, wherever it has spread, has always understood'; that is to say, the sense of the universal Church, teaching and learning that which the Fathers of the Second Council of Carthage, which concerned itself with original sin against the Pelagians, considered **a rule of faith."** —PAUL VI, ON ORIGINAL SIN, JULY, 1966

Can certain explanations of original sin given by some modern authors be reconciled with authentic Catholic doctrine?

"It is evident that the explanations of original sin given by some modern authors will seem to you irreconcilable with true Catholic doctrine. Starting from the undemonstrated premise of polygenism (origin of the human race from many couples), they deny, more or less clearly, that the sin from which so many cesspools of evil have come to mankind was first of all the disobedience of Adam, 'first man,' figure of the man to come (Church in the Modern World)—a sin committed at the beginning of history. Consequently these explanations do not even agree with the teaching of Scripture, of sacred tradition and the Church's magisterium, according to which the sin of the first man is transmitted to all his descendants not through imitation but through propagation, 'in each one as his own' and is 'the death of the soul,' that is privation and not simple lack of holiness and of justice even in new-born babies (cf. Council of Trent, 5th session, canons 2-3)."

—PAUL VI, ON ORIGINAL SIN, JULY, 1966

Did God abandon man in his fallen state?

God did not take away the hope of salvation from man, but promised a Savior, who would come in the fullness of time. In this hope, man could attain to the supernatural beatitude by observing the moral law written in his heart, which through the future merits of the Savior acquired a supernatural value.

Did God speak to humanity?

Yes, history tells us that He spoke to the first man, Adam; afterwards He spoke by means of the prophets and of the sacred writers; finally God Himself descended among men with the Incarnation of the Word to complete and fulfill revelation.

In what terms did God speak to Adam after his fall?

After the fall of Adam, God spoke to him thus: "Because you have listened to your wife, and have eaten of the tree of which I commanded you not to eat: cursed be the ground because of you; in toil shall you eat of it all the days of your life; thorns and thistles shall it bring forth to you, and you shall eat the plants of the field. In the sweat of your brow you shall eat bread, till you return to the ground, since out of it you were taken; for dust you are and unto dust you shall return" (Genesis 3:17-19).

What hopes did God give to humanity?

God promised to humanity the Redemption in His Son (Jesus Christ) with the following words: "I will put enmity between you (infernal serpent) and the woman (Mary, Mother of the Savior): between your seed and her seed (the Savior): he shall crush your head" (Genesis 3:15).

"We believe that our Lord Jesus Christ, by the sacrifice of the cross, redeemed us from original sin and all the personal sins committed by each one of us, so that, in accordance with the word of the apostle, 'where sin abounded, grace did more abound.'"

—PAUL VI, CREDO OF THE PEOPLE OF GOD

MAN INJURES HIMSELF

"Although he was made by God in a state of holiness, from the very onset of his history man abused his liberty at the urging of the

Evil One. Man set himself against God and sought to attain his goal apart from God. Although they knew God, they did not glorify Him as God, but their senseless minds were darkened and they served the creature rather than the Creator.

"What divine Revelation makes known to us agrees with experience. Examining his heart, man finds that he has inclinations toward evil too, and is engulfed by manifold ills which cannot come from his good Creator. Often refusing to acknowledge God as his beginning, man has disrupted also his proper relationship to his own ultimate goal as well as his whole relationship toward himself and others and all created things.

"Therefore man is split within himself. As a result, all of human life, whether individual or collective, shows itself to be a dramatic struggle between good and evil, between light and darkness. Indeed, man finds that by himself he is incapable of battling the assaults of evil successfully, so that everyone feels as though he is bound by chains. But the Lord Himself came to free and strengthen man, renewing him inwardly and casting out that 'prince of this world' (John 12:31) who held him in the bondage of sin. For sin has diminished man, blocking his path to fulfillment.

"The call to grandeur and the depths of misery, both of which are a part of human experience, find their ultimate and simultaneous explanation in the light of this revelation." PASTORAL CONSTITUTION ON CHURCH IN MODERN WORLD

...BUT GOD HEALS ALL

"At all times and in every race God has given welcome to whosoever fears Him and does what is right. God, however, does not make men holy and save them merely as individuals, without bond or link between one another. Rather has it pleased Him to bring men together as one people, a people which acknowledges Him in truth and serves Him in holiness. He therefore chose the race of Israel as a people unto Himself. With it He set up a covenant.

"Step by step He taught and prepared this people, making known in its history both Himself and the decree of His will and making it holy unto Himself. All these things, however, were done by way of preparation and as a figure of that new and perfect covenant, which was to be ratified in Christ, and of that fuller revelation which was to be given through the Word of God Himself made flesh.

" 'Behold the days shall come, said the Lord, and I will make a new covenant with the house of Israel, and with the house of Judah...I will give my law in their bowels, and I will write it in their heart, and I will be their God, and they shall be my people...For all of them shall know me, from the least of them even to the greatest, said the Lord.'

"Christ instituted this new covenant, the new testament, that is to say, in His blood, calling together a people made up of Jew and gentile, making them one, not according to the flesh but in the Spirit. This was to be the new People of God.

"For those who believe in Christ, who are reborn not from perishable but from an imperishable seed through the word of the living God, not from the flesh but from water and the Holy Spirit, are finally established as 'a chosen race, a royal priesthood, a holy nation, a purchased people...who in times past were not a people, but are now the people of God.'"

— DOGMATIC CONSTITUTION ON THE CHURCH

MEN OF GOD

Through the patriarchs, and after them through Moses and the prophets, God taught the Chosen People to acknowledge Himself the one, living and true God, provident father and just judge, and to wait for the Savior promised by Him, and in this manner prepared the way for the Gospel down through the centuries.
                                    —Constitution on Divine Revelation

Who were the prophets?
The prophets were God's messengers, called by Him to be spiritual leaders of the Chosen People. Through them God made known His designs to carry out the plan of salvation. The chief preoccupation of all the prophets was that of keeping the Hebrew people firmly rooted in faith in the one God and fidelity to the alliance they had made with Him.

Under divine inspiration, the prophets admonished kings and people for abandoning the way of God; threatened punishments (which always came about unless penance was done); fought sin; explained the law; and consoled the people with the promise of the coming of the Messia—"God with us," our Savior.

How many prophets were there and who were they?
We distinguish between **major** and **minor** prophets, a distinction based, mostly, on the amount of their writings. There are four major prophets: Isaia, Jeremia, Ezechiel, and Daniel. The twelve minor prophets are: Osee, Joel, Amos, Abdia, Jona, Michea, Nahum, Habacuc, Sophonia, Aggai, Zacharia and Malachia.

Who were the hagiographers?

The hagiographers were virtuous men who wrote under the inspiration of God. Therefore the books written by them have God Himself as author.

What books did they write?

There are in all 46 sacred books in the **Old Testament,** divided into: a) **historical books:** 1. Genesis; 2. Exodus; 3. Leviticus; 4. Numbers; 5. Deuteronomy; 6. Josue; 7. Judges; 8. Ruth; 9. First Samuel (Kings); 10. Second Samuel (Kings); 11. Third Book of Kings; 12. Fourth Book of Kings; 13. First Book of Paralipomenon; 14. Second Book of Paralipomenon; 15. Ezra; 16. Nehemia (Second Ezra); 17. Tobia; 18. Judith; 19. Esther; 20. First Book of Machabees; 21. Second Book of Machabees; b) **didactic books:** 22. Job; 23. Psalms; 24. Proverbs; 25. Ecclesiastes; 26. Canticle of Canticles; 27. Wisdom; 28. Sirach (Ecclesiasticus); c) **prophetic books:** 29. Isaia, 30. Jeremia; 31. Lamentations; 32. Baruch; 33. Ezechiel; 34. Daniel; 35. Osee; 36. Joel; 37. Amos; 38. Abdia; 39. Jona; 40. Michea; 41. Nahum; 42. Habacuc; 43. Sophonia; 44. Aggai; 45. Zacharia; 46. Malachia.

How are we certain that the writings of the prophets and the hagiographers are truly inspired by God?

That the writings of the prophets and of the hagiographers are truly inspired by God is assured us by many reasons of an internal and external nature. The reasons of an internal nature are: immunity from error, from contradiction and from fraud; in addition the perfect conformity to right reason and to history, their excellence in themselves and in effects. Of particular importance, and a basis of absolute certainty are the reasons of an external nature, that is, **miracles** and **prophecies.**

What is a miracle?

A miracle is a sensible, extraordinary fact, superior to all the powers and the laws of nature and therefore such that it can only come from God, author and master of nature.

Is a miracle possible?

A miracle is possible, admitting the existence and omnipotence of God. Just as He has established laws, He can also suspend them.

Do miracles really prove a truth?

Miracles show the intervention of God: they are therefore most certain and clear signs of a truth; God cannot approve the false.

How can a miracle be considered?

A miracle can be considered under the historical, philosophical and theological aspect. It must be historically verified, it must transcend every natural causality and must implicitly or explicitly demonstrate divine action. Example: the three youths in the burning furnace (see Book of Daniel). The fact is historically certain; the causes cannot be natural; the end was that of demonstrating that the God honored by the Hebrews was the only true God.

How many kinds of miracles are there?
Miracles are of three kinds: 1) physical miracles: e.g., the resurrection of a dead person; 2) intellectual miracles: e.g., a prophecy; 3) moral miracles: e.g., the heroism of martyrs, especially if children.

What is prophecy?
Prophecy is the explicit and certain prediction of a future event not naturally foreseeable.

Does prophecy show the intervention of God?
Prophecy, being "knowledge of a truth which it is naturally impossible to foresee," is a certain proof of the intervention of God when it is confirmed by events.

Is the revelation of the Old Testament confirmed by miracles and prophecies?
In the Old Testament miracles and prophecies abound. It is sufficient to remember the miracles worked by Moses, by the Prophets Elia, Daniel, Eliseus, etc. Among the prophecies, the most celebrated concern the coming of the Messiah, His life, His death and His glory.

Did Jesus Christ acknowledge the Old Testament?
Yes. In fact He showed how all the ancient prophecies were being fulfilled in Him, as is seen from the Holy Gospel. Example: "Today this Scripture has been fulfilled in your hearing" (Luke 4:21). "Search the Scriptures... they bear witness to me" (John 5:39).

How did the expectation of the Messiah begin and grow in the Old Testament?

1) God announced the Redeemer to Adam. 2) In Genesis it appears that the Savior will come from the Semitic race, will descend from the posterity of Abraham, will come from the tribe of Juda. 3) He will be of the family of David. 4) He will be born of a Virgin, at Bethlehem, in a specified time. 5) He will teach the people; He will be the Man of sorrows. Put to death, He will arise glorious and will establish a kingdom above all kingdoms, which will not have an end (the Church).

THE SACRED SCRIPTURES

"Every day I read the Bible, and I will read it as long as my eyes will be able to read it. I will read it everywhere: in the light of the sun and of the fireplace, in full day and in full night, in joy and in sorrow, in health and in sickness, in days of hope and in those of doubt, in enthusiasm and in depression of spirit. Each time it seems to me that I have read something completely new and unknown until then."

— MERESCHKOWKI

THE OLD TESTAMENT

"In carefully planning and preparing the salvation of the whole human race the God of infinite love, by a special dispensation, chose for Himself a people to whom He would entrust His promises. First He entered into a covenant with Abraham (see Genesis 15:18) and, through

Moses, with the people of Israel (see Exodus 24:8). To this people which He had acquired for Himself, He so manifested Himself through words and deeds as the one true and living God that Israel came to know by experience the ways of God with men. Then too, when God Himself spoke to them through the mouth of the prophets, Israel daily gained a deeper and clearer understanding of His ways and made them more widely known among the nations (see Psalms 21:29; 95:1-3; Isaia 2:1-5; Jeremia 3:17).

"The plan of salvation foretold by the sacred authors, recounted and explained by them, is found as the true word of God in the books of the Old Testament: these books, therefore, written under divine inspiration, remain permanently valuable. 'For all that was written for our instruction, so that by the steadfastness and the encouragement of the Scriptures we might have hope' (Romans 15:4).

"The principal purpose to which the plan of the old covenant was directed was to prepare for the coming of Christ, the redeemer of all and of the messianic kingdom, to announce this coming by prophecy (see Luke 24:44; John 5:39; 1 Peter 1:10), and to indicate its meaning through various types (see 1 Corinthians 10:12). Now the books of the Old Testament, in accordance with the state of mankind before the time of salvation established by Christ, reveal to all men the knowledge of God and of man and the ways in which God, just and merciful, deals with men.

"These books, though they also contain some things which are incomplete and temporary, nevertheless show us true divine pedagogy. These same books, then, give expression to a lively sense of God, contain a store of sublime teachings about God, sound wisdom about human life, and a wonderful treasury of prayers, and in them the mystery of our salvation is present in a hidden way. Christians should receive them with reverence.

"God, the inspirer and author of both Testaments, wisely arranged that the New Testament be hidden in the Old and the Old be made manifest in the New. For, though Christ established the new covenant in His blood (see Luke 22:20; 1 Corinthians 11:25), still the books of the Old Testament with all their parts, caught up into the proclamation of the Gospel, acquire and show forth their full meaning in the New Testament (see Matthew 5:17; Luke 24:27; Romans 16:25-26; 2 Corinthians 14:16) and in turn shed light on it and explain it."   — DOGMATIC CONSTITUTION ON DIVINE REVELATION

WHO IS JESUS CHRIST?

God so loved the world that he gave his only-begotten Son, that those who believe in him may not perish, but may have life everlasting. —John 3:16

God who "wills that all men be saved and come to the knowledge of the truth" (1 Timothy 2:4), "who in many and various ways spoke in times past to the fathers by the prophets" (Hebrews 1:1), when the fullness of time had come sent His Son, the Word made flesh, anointed by the Holy Spirit, to preach the Gospel to the poor, to heal the contrite of heart, to be a bodily and spiritual medicine, the Mediator between God and man. For His humanity, united with the person of the Word, was the instrument of our salvation. Therefore in Christ the perfect achievement of our reconciliation came forth, and the fullness of divine worship was given to us.

The wonderful works of God among the people of the Old Testament were but a prelude to the work of Christ the Lord in redeeming mankind and giving perfect glory to God.

— Constitution on Sacred Liturgy

Jesus Christ was sent into the world as a real mediator between God and men. Since He is God, all divine fullness dwells bodily in Him (cf. Colossians 2:9). According to His human nature, on the other hand, He is the new Adam, made head of a renewed humanity, and full of grace and truth (John 1:14). Therefore the Son of God walked the ways of a true Incarnation that He might make men sharers in the nature of God.

— Decree on Mission Activity of Church

81

What does Revelation teach concerning God?
Revelation teaches us that there exists one true God in three Divine Persons equal and distinct: Father, Son and Holy Spirit.

What is the Incarnation?
The Incarnation is the assumption of a human nature by the second Person of the Blessed Trinity, who thus, remaining true God, also became true man; He is called Jesus Christ.

Who is Jesus Christ?
Christ is the Son of God incarnate, who made Himself our Master, Priest and Victim. In this manner He redeemed humanity from error, from vice, from idolatry and from atheism.

How did Jesus Christ show that He was true God?
Jesus Christ showed that He was true God: 1) by fulfilling in Himself the ancient prophecies which announced Him as the Messias; 2) by His admirable doctrine, superior to all others; 3) by His most holy life; 4) by His testimony confirmed by miracles, above all the miracle of His resurrection; 5) by the heroic testimony rendered to Him by the martyrs; 6) by the rapid diffusion of His

The most complete
definition Jesus gave
Himself is
I am
the Way,
the Truth
and the Life.

doctrine and by the restoration brought about by Him in the individual, in the family, in society.

What are some scriptural proofs of the divinity of Jesus Christ?

Some of these proofs are:

From His miracles:

He raised Himself from the dead

"... They found the stone rolled back from the tomb. But on entering, they did not find the body of the Lord Jesus. And it came to pass, while they were wondering what to make of this, that, behold, two men stood by them in dazzling raiment. And when the women were struck with fear and bowed their faces to the ground, they said to them, 'Why do you seek the living one among the dead? He is not here, but has risen' (Luke 14:1-6).

He ruled the natural elements

"And do you not remember when I broke the five loaves among five thousand... and when I broke the seven loaves among four thousand?" (Mark 8:18-20)

He cured the sick

"Go and report to John what you have heard and seen: the blind see, the lame walk, the lepers are cleansed, the deaf hear!" (Matthew 11:4-5).

He raised the dead

"Young man, I say to you, arise" (Luke 7:14).
"Girl, arise" (Luke 8:54).
"Lazarus, come forth!" (John 11:43)

He cast out devils

Now when it was evening, they brought to him many who were possessed, and he cast out the spirits with a word (Matthew 8:16).

From His prophecies:

He predicted His own passion and resurrection

"Behold, we are going up to Jerusalem, and the Son of Man will be betrayed to the chief priests and the Scribes; and they will condemn him to death, and will deliver him to the Gentiles to be mocked and scourged and crucified; and on the third day he will rise again" (Mt. 20:18-19).

He predicted Peter's denial

"Amen I say to you, today, this very night, before a cock crows twice, you will deny me three times" (Mark 14:30).

He predicted Judas' betrayal

"Amen, amen, I say to you, one of you will betray me" (John 13:21).

He predicted the destruction of the temple

"Amen I say to you, there will not be left here one stone upon another that will not be thrown down" (Matthew 24:2).

From His own testimony:

to Nicodemus

"And no one has ascended into heaven except him who has descended from heaven: the Son of Man who is in heaven" (John 3:13).

to the Samaritan woman

"I who speak with you am he (the Messiah) (John 4:26).

to the Scribes and Pharisees

"...he called God his own Father, making himself equal to God" (John 5:18).

"For from God I came forth and have come" (John 8:42).

"Amen, amen, I say to you, before Abraham came to be, I am" (John 8:58).

to the Sanhedrin

"You have said it (I am the Messiah, the Son of God) (Matthew 26:64).

to the people

"I and the Father are one" (John 10:30).

"...him who is from God, he has seen the Father" (John 6:46).

to His disciples

"Do you believe that I am in the Father, and the Father in me?" (John 14:11)

The testimony of the Father:

at the Jordan

And behold, a voice from the heavens said, "This is my beloved Son, in whom I am well pleased." (Mt. 3:17)

on Tabor

As he was still speaking, behold, a bright cloud overshadowed them, and behold, a voice out of the cloud said, "This is my beloved Son, in whom I am well pleased; hear him" (Mt. 17:5).

in the Temple

There came therefore a voice from heaven, "I have both glorified it, and I will glorify it again" (John 12:28).

The testimony of the demons:

in Galilee

...an unclean spirit cried out, saying, "What have we to do with you, Jesus of Nazareth? Have you come to destroy us? I know who you are, the Holy One of God" (Mark 1:23-24).

And the unclean spirits, whenever they beheld him, fell down before him and cried out, saying, "You are the Son of God" (Mark 3:11).

in the Decapolis

And when he (the unclean spirit) saw Jesus, he fell down before him, and crying out with a loud voice said, "What have I to do with you, Jesus, Son of the most high God? I pray you, do not torment me" (Luke 8:28).

The testimony of the Jewish people:

Simeon

"My eyes have seen your salvation" (Lk. 2:30).

Martha

"Yes, Lord, I believe that you are the Christ, the Son of God, come into the world" (John 11:27).

the people

"This is indeed the Prophet who is to come into the world" (John 6:14).

"He has done all things well. He has made both the deaf to hear and the dumb to speak" (Mark 7:37).

"Never did we see the like" (Mark 2:12).

"A great prophet has risen among us. God has visited his people" (Luke 7:16).

"When the Christ comes will he work more signs than this man works?" (John 7:31).

"Never has man spoken as this man" (John 7:46).

"Hosanna! Blessed is he who comes in the name of the Lord, the king of Israel!" (John 12:13).

The testimony of the disciples:

John the Baptist

"Behold the Lamb of God, who takes away the sins of the world" (John 1:29).

"After me there comes one who has been set above me, because he was before me" (John 1:30).

Andrew

"We have found the Messiah" (John 1:41).

Philip

"We have found him of whom Moses in the law and the prophets wrote, Jesus the son of Joseph of Nazareth" (John 1:45).

Nathanael

"Rabbi, you are the Son of God, you are the King of Israel" (John 1:49).

Peter

"Lord, to whom shall we go? You have words of everlasting life, and we have come to believe and to know that you are the Christ, the Son of God" (John 6:69-70).

"You are the Christ, the Son of the living God" (Matthew 16:16).

Thomas

"My Lord and my God!" (John 20:28)

How can we be sure that Christ really died on Calvary?

Let us recall the Gospel narrative that treats of

His passion. The first step in His passion was the agony in the garden, where He suffered so intensely that His blood burst through arteries and veins and blanketed His sacred body in red. It was a death agony: "My soul is sorrowful even unto death."

He was next subjected to a night of horrors by His tormentors. Then came the cruel scourging followed by the tortures inflicted upon Him by the soldiery during the night of His imprisonment. After His trial before Pilate there came His most sorrowful journey to Calvary bearing the cross. The crucifixion ended the long trial of torments and crushed out the last spark of life. The executioners did not break the legs of their Victim because they saw that He had died. A Roman spear thrust into the Sacred Heart made His death certain beyond the shadow of a doubt.

If all the tortures He suffered did not bring about death, certainly His mother and His friends who looked after His burial would have discovered that they were handling a living body. Lastly we have His own sacred testimony that He died and rose from the tomb. °

How can we be sure that Christ truly rose from the dead?
Four conflicting explanations have been offered for Christ's empty tomb. First, He was not dead but in a swoon. He regained consciousness and escaped from the grave. Secondly, the body could have been swallowed up during the earth-

° Rev. Peter Sullivan, *Christ the Answer*, St. Paul Ed., 1964.

quake. Thirdly, the apostles might have stolen the body. Finally, Christ rose from the dead by His own power and consequently He is God as He said.

The swoon theory is impossible, for no one undergoing the hours of tortures that Christ experienced could possibly avoid dying. The earthquake theory is faulty because if the earthquake swallowed the body, the linen cloths and the napkin should have been swallowed too. To suppose that the apostles could have stolen the body with the tomb guarded by a platoon of soldiers is surely a flimsy supposition. Moreover a study of the characters of Christ's apostles show them to be timid, ignorant men who would have been incapable of thinking out such a plan or of executing it.° The only possible explanation, therefore, is that Christ really rose from the dead and consequently He is God, as He claimed.

How did Jesus Christ define Himself?

Jesus gave Himself various definitions. The most complete is the following: "I am the Way, the Truth and the Life."

How did the Son of God-made-man speak to humanity?

1) First of all the Son of God confirmed the doctrine, the prophecies and the moral teaching already announced by God by means of Moses and the other hagiographers and prophets in the Old Testament. 2) He confirmed

---

° Rev. Peter Sullivan, *Christ the Answer*, St. Paul Ed., 1964.

and explained the natural and divine law by applying it to many cases. 3) He added many doctrinal teachings, among which are deep mysteries, e.g., the mystery of the Most Holy Trinity, that is, one God in three Persons; and many moral teachings capable of leading us to the highest perfection. 4) He pointed out to men the way of salvation and of sanctity with the example of His most holy life. 5) He instituted the Church which is the teacher to men of all times and of all places.

Where is the doctrine of Jesus Christ contained?
The doctrine of Christ was partly written in the books of the New Testament and partly passed on by word of mouth, which constitutes Sacred Tradition.

What are the sacred books of the New Testament?
The New Testament contains 27 sacred Books: 1) the four texts of the one Gospel of Jesus Christ, according to St. Matthew, St. Mark, St. Luke and St. John; 2) the Acts of the Apostles; 3) the Letters of the Apostles: of which 14 are of St. Paul, two of St. Peter, three of St. John, one of St. James, one of St. Jude; 4) the prophetic book called the Apocalypse or Revelation.

Are the Gospels true historical documents?
We can prove them so if we can prove three things: 1) That the recorded facts actually occurred. 2) That they were faithfully reported. 3) That they have come down to us substantially as they were written in the beginning. *

---

* Rev. Peter Sullivan, *Christ the Answer*, St. Paul Ed., 1964.

Did the Gospel facts occur?
Unless the evangelists lied or were the victims of their own imagination, the facts occurred as recounted. If the writers lied, they would have been denounced by their contemporaries, many of whom witnessed the events in the life of Christ. And surely if the writers were bent on deception, they would not have revealed their own weaknesses, nor would they have proclaimed the lofty moral standards of Christ's teaching.

The authors of the Gospel message continually show too much common sense to be the victims of a delusion. Finally acceptance of the Gospel message down through the centuries by millions of people of every class, tribe and tongue even at the cost of life, is a phenomenon that could not rest on a lie.°

Were the Gospel facts faithfully reported?
Yes—internal evidence proves it so. The authors prove themselves to be contemporaries of Christ, familiar with His life and teaching. They draw a picture of Palestine with every detail of local color that we know is accurate from other historical sources. The message itself then proves that the writers were sincere men, anxious as good journalists to record the events that happened. °

Have the Gospel facts reached us substantially as they were recorded?
Scientific investigation by the hostile school of higher criticism proves that. The whole purpose

---

° Rev. Peter Sullivan, *Christ the Answer*, St. Paul Ed., 1964.

of this school of higher criticism was to show that the Gospel message was a myth. But on the contrary, its own findings showed the Gospels to be genuine history. There is no more reason to doubt the accuracy of the life of Christ than to doubt the life of Julius Caesar. °

What is the Bible?
The 46 books of the Old Testament and the 27 of the New constitute Sacred Scripture, popularly called the **Holy Bible,** which means **book** par excellence or divine.

Why should the Bible be read and to whom are its words addressed?
The Bible is the book of shepherd and flock alike; it is the Book for all. May it become our daily bread. If we read what God has written, we will think according to God. The Bible is the Lord's letter inviting us to heaven, the communication of His secrets and His designs concerning us.

How should the Bible be read?
The Bible should be read with humility and faith. "Prayer should accompany the reading of Sacred Scripture, so that God and man may talk together."   – DOGMATIC CONSTITUTION ON DIVINE REVELATION

What is Sacred Tradition?
Sacred Tradition is revealed doctrine which concerns faith and morals, not written in the Bible, but infallibly transmitted from age to age, especially by means of the Shepherds of the Church.

° Rev. Peter Sullivan, *Christ the Answer*, St. Paul Ed., 1964.

What value does Sacred Tradition have?
Divine Tradition, preserved and taught by the magisterium of the Church, is a font of Revelation, distinct from the Scriptures but like Sacred Scripture infallible.

What are the organs of Tradition?
Organs of Tradition are the Pope, the bishops, the Fathers of the Church, and therefore the dogmatic definitions, the ordinary magisterium, the creeds and the professions of faith, sacred liturgies, sacred monuments, the practices of the Church, etc.

JESUS REVEALED GOD THE FATHER TO US

"If I had not known the Christ, God would have been for me a meaningless word; the Infinite Being would have been unimaginable to me. If the Christ had not said: **Our Father,** I would never have had by myself the sense of this filial relationship; this invocation would never have risen from my heart to my lips."

— FRANCOIS MAURIAC

THE SACRED SCRIPTURES

"I confess that the majesty of the Scriptures amazes me and the sanctity of the Gospel speaks to my heart; see how, on the contrary, the books of the philosophers with all their pomp, are insignificant in comparison to it! Can it ever be possible that a book at the same time so sublime and so simple be the work of men?... That the evangelical work be an invention? It is not thus that one invents!

Hebrew authors could never have known how to find that tone and that moral teaching; the Gospel has characters of truth so great, so touching, and so perfectly inimitable that the inventor would be greater than a hero."

—JEAN JACQUES ROUSSEAU

THE NEW TESTAMENT

"The word of God, which is the power of God for the salvation of all who believe (cf. Romans 1:16), is set forth and shows its power in a most excellent way in the writings of the New Testament. For when the fullness of time arrived (cf. Galatians 4:4), the Word was made flesh and dwelt among us in His fullness of graces and truth (cf. John 1:14). Christ established the kingdom of God on earth, manifested His Father and Himself by deeds and words, and completed His work by His death, resurrection and glorious Ascension and by the sending of the Holy Spirit. Having been lifted up from the earth, He draws all men to Himself (cf. John 12:32, Greek text), He who alone has the words of eternal life (cf. John 6:68).

"This mystery had not been manifested to other generations as it was now revealed to His holy Apostles and prophets in the Holy Spirit (cf. Ephesians 3:4-6, Greek text), so that they might preach the Gospel, stir up faith in Jesus, Christ and Lord, and gather together the Church. Now the writings of the New Testament stand as a perpetual and divine witness to these realities.

"It is common knowledge that among all the Scriptures, even those of the New Testament, the Gospels have a special pre-eminence, and rightly so, for they are the principal witness for the life and teaching of the incarnate Word, our savior.

"The Church has always and everywhere held and continues to hold that the four Gospels are of apostolic origin. For what the Apostles preached in fulfillment of the commission of Christ, afterwards they themselves and apostolic men, under the inspiration of the divine Spirit, handed on to us in writing: the foundation of faith, namely, the fourfold Gospel, according to Matthew, Mark, Luke and John.

"Holy Mother Church has firmly and with absolute constancy held, and continues to hold, that the four Gospels just named, whose historical character the Church unhesitatingly asserts, faithfully hand on what Jesus Christ, while living among men, really did and taught for their eternal salvation until the day He was taken up into heaven (cf. Acts 1:1). Indeed, after the Ascension of the Lord the Apostles handed on to their hearers what He had said and done. This they did with that clearer understanding which they enjoyed after they had been instructed by the glorious events of Christ's life and taught by the light of the Spirit of truth.

"The sacred authors wrote the four Gospels, selecting some things from the many which had been handed on by word of mouth or in writing, reducing some of them to a synthesis, explaining some things in view of the situation of their churches, and preserving the form of proclamation but always in such fashion that they told us the honest truth about Jesus. For their intention in writing was that either from their own memory and recollections, or from the witness of those who 'themselves from the beginning were eye witnesses and ministers of the Word' we might know 'the truth' concerning those matters about which we have been instructed (cf. Luke 1:2-4).

"Besides the four Gospels, the canon of the New Testament also contains the epistles of St. Paul and other apostolic writings, composed under the inspiration of the Holy Spirit, by which, according to the wise plan of God, those matters which concern Christ the Lord are confirmed, His true teaching is more and more fully stated, the saving power of the divine work of Christ is preached, the story is told of the beginnings of the Church and its marvelous growth, and its glorious fulfillment is foretold.

"For the Lord Jesus was with His apostles as He had promised (cf. Matthew 28:20) and sent them the advocate Spirit who would lead them into the fullness of truth'' (cf. John 16:13). — DOGMATIC CONSTITUTION ON DIVINE REVELATION

SACRED TRADITION

"In order to keep the Gospel forever whole and alive within the Church, the apostles left bishops as their successors, handing over to them the authority to teach in their own place. This Sacred Tradition, therefore, and Sacred Scripture of both the Old and New Testaments are like a mirror in which the pilgrim Church on earth looks at God, from whom she has received everything, until she is brought finally to see Him as He is, face to face (cf. 1 John 3:2).

"And so the apostolic preaching, which is expressed in a special way in the inspired books, was to be preserved by an unending succession of preachers until the end of time. Therefore the apostles, handing on what they themselves had received, warn the faithful to hold fast to the traditions which they have learned either by word of mouth or by letter (cf. 2 Thessalonians 2:15), and to fight in defense of the faith handed on once and for all (cf. Jude 1:3).

"Now what was handed on by the apostles includes everything which contributes toward the holiness of life and increase in faith of the People of God; and so the Church, in her teaching, life and worship, perpetuates and hands on to all generations all that she herself is, all that she believes.

"This Tradition which comes from the apostles develops in the Church with the help of the Holy Spirit. For there is a growth in the understanding of the realities and the words which have been handed down. This happens through the contemplation and study made by believers, who treasure these things in their hearts (cf. Luke 2:19, 51) through a penetrating understanding of the spiritual realities which they experience, and through the preaching of those who have received through episcopal succession the sure gift of truth. For as the centuries succeed one another, the Church constantly moves forward toward the fullness of divine truth until the words of God reach their complete fulfillment in her.

"The words of the holy fathers witness to the presence of this living Tradition, whose wealth is poured into the practice and life of the believing and praying Church. Through the same Tradition the Church's full canon of the sacred books is known, and the sacred writings themselves are more profoundly understood and unceasingly made active in her; and thus God, who spoke of old, uninterruptedly converses with the bride of His beloved Son; and the Holy Spirit, through whom the living voice of the Gospel resounds in the Church, and through her, in the world, leads unto all truth those who believe and makes the word of Christ dwell abundantly in them (cf. Colossians 3:16).

"Hence there exists a close connection and communication between Sacred Tradition and Sacred Scripture. For both of them, flowing from the same divine wellspring, in a certain way merge into a unity and tend toward the same end. For Sacred Scripture is the word of God inasmuch as it is consigned to writing under the inspiration of the divine Spirit, while Sacred Tradition takes the word of God entrusted by Christ the Lord and the Holy Spirit to the apostles, and hands it on to their successors in its full purity, so that led by the light of the Spirit of truth, they may in proclaiming it preserve this word of God faithfully, explain it, and make it more widely known. Consequently it is not from Sacred Scripture alone that the Church draws her certainty about everything which has been revealed.

"Therefore both Sacred Tradition and Sacred Scripture are to be accepted and venerated with the same sense of loyalty and reverence."

— DOGMATIC CONSTITUTION ON DIVINE REVELATION

GOD HAS SPOKEN

"God, who at sundry times and in divers manners spoke in times past to the fathers by the prophets, last of all in these days **has spoken to us by his Son,** whom he appointed heir of all things, by whom also he made the world" (Hebrews 1:1-2).

"Then he began to reproach the towns in which most of his miracles were worked, because they had not repented. 'Woe to you, Corozain! woe to you, Bethsaida! For if in Tyre and Sidon had been worked the miracles that have been worked in you, they would have repented long ago in sackcloth and ashes. But I tell you, it will be more tolerable for Tyre and Sidon on the day of judgment than for you. And you,

Capharnaum, shall you be exalted to heaven? You shall be thrust down to hell! For if the miracles had been worked in Sodom that have been worked in you, it would have remained to this day. But I tell you, it will be more tolerable for the land of Sodom on the day of judgment than for you.'

"At that time Jesus spoke and said, 'I praise you, Father, Lord of heaven and earth, that you hide these things from the wise and prudent, and reveal them to little ones. Yes, Father, for such was your good pleasure'" (Matthew 11:20-26).

"God's Word, by whom all things were made, was Himself made flesh so that as perfect man He might save all men and sum up all things in Himself. The Lord is the goal of human history, the focal point of the longings of history and of civilization, the center of the human race, the joy of every heart and the answer to all its yearnings. He it is Whom the Father raised from the dead, lifted on high and stationed at His right hand, making Him judge of the living and the dead. Enlivened and united in His Spirit, we journey toward the consummation of human history, one which fully accords with the counsel of God's love: 'To re-establish all things in Christ, both those in the heavens and those on the earth' (Ephesians 11:10)."

—PASTORAL CONSTITUTION ON CHURCH IN MODERN WORLD

FOLLOWERS OF
JESUS CHRIST

*No one is freed from sin by himself and by his own power,
no one is raised above himself, no one is completely rid
of his sickness or his solitude or his servitude. On the
contrary, all stand in need of Christ, their model, their
mentor, their liberator, their Savior, their source of life.*
        —Decree on Mission Activity of Church

Why did the Son of God become man?

The Son of God became man to make reparation for the sin of our first parents, who, by their sin, had lost for themselves and for all their descendants the special gifts of God, above all, His holy grace, and with it the right to heaven.

How did Jesus Christ remedy the sin of the first man?

Jesus Christ regained for man grace, which He bestows in Baptism and in the other sacraments; He cured ignorance by revealing sublime doctrines; He cured concupiscence by offering special divine helps; He remedied death by announcing the final resurrection, thus making His mercy abound.

In what manner did the Redeemer make His mercy abound?

The Redeemer made His mercy abound in several ways: 1) with the institution of the sacraments and especially of the Holy Eucharist, by which man participates in the very life of God; 2) by giving to man the maximum sign of love with His death on the cross;

3) by indicating to us with doctrine and with example the way of perfect sanctity, summed up in the two precepts of love; 4) by opening the treasures of Revelation which allow us to know the sublimest mysteries; 5) by instituting the Church, dispenser of His treasures and continuator of His work.

What dignity did the redemption add to man's natural human dignity?

"Every human being is a person, that is, his nature is endowed with intelligence and free will. Indeed, precisely because he is a person he has rights and obligations flowing directly and simultaneously from his very nature. And as these rights and obligations are universal and inviolable, so they cannot in any way be surrendered.

"If we look upon the dignity of the human person in the light of divinely revealed truth, we cannot help but esteem it far more highly; for men are redeemed by the blood of Jesus Christ; they are by grace the children and friends of God, heirs of eternal glory."

— JOHN XXIII, PEACE ON EARTH

What does it mean to be a Christian?

A Christian is one who believes, loves, and follows Jesus Christ and lives by His very life.

What higher life does a Christian possess?

Besides being composed of soul and body, he possesses in himself divine or supernatural life, which makes him a son of God and an heir of heaven.

What does it mean to be a true follower of Jesus Christ?

"The Lord Jesus, the divine Teacher and Model of all perfection, preached holiness of life to each and every one of His disciples of every condition.... The followers of Christ are called by God, not because of their works, but according to His own purpose and grace. They are justified in the Lord Jesus, because in the baptism of faith they truly become sons of God and sharers in the divine nature. In this way they are really made holy. Then too, by God's gift, they must hold on to and complete in their lives this holiness they have received. They are warned by the Apostle to live 'as becomes saints,' and to put on 'as God's chosen ones, holy and beloved, a heart of mercy, kindness, humility, meekness, patience,' and to possess the fruit of the Spirit in holiness. Since truly we all offend in many things we all need God's mercies continually and we all must daily pray: 'Forgive us our debts....'

"All the faithful of Christ of whatever rank or status, are called to the fullness of the Christian life and to the perfection of charity.... In order that the faithful may reach this perfection, they must use their strength accordingly as they have received it, as a gift from Christ. They must follow in His footsteps and conform themselves to His image seeking the will of the Father in all things. They must devote themselves with all their being to the glory of God and the service of their neighbor....

"Every person must walk unhesitatingly according to his own personal gifts and duties in the path of living faith, which arouses hope and works through charity."

— DOGMATIC CONSTITUTION ON THE CHURCH

Thus, a true follower of Jesus Christ is one who believes the Holy Gospel, receives the sacraments well, and lives by the law of love for God and neighbor. In particular, he fulfills his obligations to his family, gives good example in society and takes part in the lay apostolate of the Church.

Can the whole of Christianity be reduced to loving our neighbor?

"It is enough to ask a certain number of persons what Christianity consists of and many will answer: 'Christianity consists in loving our neighbor.' This answer is true, since it is true that love of one's neighbor is part of Christian doctrine. But it is completely false to maintain that love of one's neighbor is the **whole** of Christianity. This means reducing Christianity to what today is defined horizontally—a word I do not like very much—that is, in Christianity there is seen only the horizontal dimension, the relationship with others, completely eliminating the vertical dimension, that is, the relationship with God."

— JEAN CARDINAL DANIELOU, CHRISTIAN FAITH AND TODAY'S MAN

"Many of the contemporary so-called theologies of hope are nothing other than veiled forms of secular humanism. They are based on the unrealistic foundation that if only we have good will, if only we love one another, if only we work together for what is good for us all, we can make a paradise out of this world. And the words of the Psalmist have never been more true: 'Unless God builds the house, they labor in vain who build it; unless God guard the gates, they watch in vain who stand guard' (Psalm 126)."

—JOHN CARDINAL CARBERRY, NEED FOR ORTHODOX CATHOLIC TEACHING

What is the error of secular humanism?

"No one can doubt that the goals which this secular humanism sets for itself are good . . . the elimination of war, and poverty, and discrimination, and hatred, and suffering that can be relieved by the scientific and humanitarian ingenuity of man. Indeed, no one can be a true Christian unless he devote himself to the attainment of these goals, because they are essential to the fulfillment of Christ's command: 'Thou Shalt Love Thy Neighbor As Thyself.'

"But agnostic secular humanism, which may be called the loving of our neighbor without the love of God, or the program for changing the world without the benefit of guidance from God or of any motive that transcends the present, will never succeed because it does not recognize man for what he is: a creature made immortal in the image and likeness of God; a creature needing redemption from sin

The concept of the divinity,
of the superior order,
of a future life...
is the balm of every
suffering soul,
transfixed and tried
every day by fatigue
and misfortune.

Guy Baccelli

through the Precious Blood of Jesus Christ; a creature to whom God has revealed Himself in Christ, who, in turn, reveals His will to the end of time through the Church He founded; a creature destined to attain by his cooperation with the redeeming grace of Christ and obedience to His will an everlasting communion with God."

—JOHN CARDINAL CARBERRY, NEED FOR ORTHODOX CATHOLIC TEACHING

How, then, should a Christian regard the building up of the world?

"Far from thinking that works produced by man's own talent and energy are in opposition to God's power, and that the rational creature exists as a kind of rival to the Creator, Christians are convinced that the triumphs of the human race are a sign of God's grace and the flowering of His own mysterious design. For the greater man's power becomes, the farther his individual and community responsibility extends."

—PASTORAL CONSTITUTION ON CHURCH IN MODERN WORLD

Are we obliged to follow Jesus Christ?

We are obliged to follow Jesus Christ because He is the Son of God, sent by the Father to teach us the way to return to Him; and hence the religion taught by Him is the only true religion.

Why is Christianity the only true religion?

Christianity is the only true religion because it is in conformity with reason and because it alone has been revealed by God Himself in historical reality: before Christ with a long period of preparation it was foretold by means of the prophets; with Christ, Son of God incarnate, it was revealed in its fullness and signed with the seal of divinity; after Christ it was testified to by the apostles and by their successors who constitute the infallible magisterium of the Church.

Does the Christian have a duty to spread his faith?

"The Christian vocation by its very nature is also a vocation to the apostolate. No part of the structure of a living body is merely passive but has a share in the functions as well as life of the body: so, too, in the body of Christ, which is the Church, 'the whole body . . . in keeping with the proper activity of each part, derives its increase from its own internal development' (Ephesians 4:16).

"Indeed, the organic union in this body and the structure of the members are so compact that the member who fails to make his proper contribution to the development of the Church must be said to be useful neither to the Church nor to himself."

— DECREE ON APOSTOLATE OF LAITY

"The time has come when the laity must take their places by the side of their consecrated leaders in the urgent task of bringing the teachings of Christ to those who know Him not. This is the most urgent task facing our laity."

— PIUS XII

"Each one...must be zealous for the spiritual welfare of his neighbor, for the defense of his own Faith, to make it known to him who is completely ignorant of it, or to him who knows it imperfectly."

—JOHN XXIII

Upon what does a fruitful apostolate depend?

"Since Christ, sent by the Father, is the source and origin of the whole apostolate of the Church, the success of the lay apostolate depends on the laity's living union with Christ, in keeping with the Lord's words, 'He who abides in me, and I in him, bears much fruit for without me you can do nothing.'"

DECREE ON APOSTOLATE OF LAITY

Why is the apostolate of communications important?

"Press, radio, television and motion pictures have a particular importance—owing to their close and mutual relationships, and pose in our times problems so grave as to influence not only culture, civilization and public morality, but religion itself. Therefore they require today not only a particular solicitude on the part of the holy pastors and an efficacious presence of the faithful, but also the active collaboration of all men of good will."

—PAUL VI, MOTU PROPRIO IN FRUCTIBUS

What does the communications apostolate involve?

"All the children of the Church should join, without delay and with the greatest effort in a common work to make effective use of the media of social communication in various apostolic endeavors, as circumstances and conditions demand. They should anticipate harmful developments, especially in regions where more urgent efforts to advance morality and religion are needed....

"The laity who have something to do with the use of these media should endeavor to bear witness to Christ, first of all by carrying out their individual duties or office expertly and with an apostolic spirit, and, further, by being of direct help in the pastoral activity of the Church—to the best of their ability—through their technical, economic, cultural and artistic talents.

"Good journalism should be fostered. To instill a fully Christian spirit into readers, a truly Catholic press should be set up and encouraged. Such a press—whether immediately fostered and directed by ecclesiastical authorities or by Catholic laymen—should be edited with the clear purpose of forming, supporting and advancing public opinion in accord with natural law and Catholic teaching and precepts. It should disseminate and properly explain news concerning the life of the Church. Moreover, the faithful ought to be advised of the necessity both to spread and read the Catholic press to formulate Christian judgments for themselves on all events.

"The production and showing of films that have value as decent entertainment, humane culture or art, especially when they are designed for young people, ought to be encouraged and assured by every effective means. This can be done particularly by supporting and joining in projects and enterprises for the production and distribution of decent films, by encouraging worthwhile films through critical approval and awards, by patronizing or jointly sponsoring theaters operated by Catholic and responsible managers.

"Similarly, effective support should be given to good radio and television programs, above all those that are suitable for families. Catholic programs should be promoted, in which listeners and viewers can be brought to share in the life of the Church and learn religious truths. An effort should also be made, where it may be necessary, to set up Catholic stations. In such instances, however, care must be taken that their programs are outstanding for their standards of excellence and achievement."

— DECREE ON MEDIA OF SOCIAL COMMUNICATION

Who are obliged to insure the morality of the media?

"For the proper use of these media, it is most necessary that all who employ them be acquainted with the norms of morality and conscientiously put them into practice in this area. They must look, then, to the nature of what is communicated, given the special character of each of these media. At the same time they must take into consideration the entire situation or circumstances, namely, the persons, place, time and other conditions under which communication takes place and which can affect or totally change its propriety. Among these circumstances to be considered is the precise manner in which a given medium achieves its effect. For its influence can be so great that men, especially if they are unprepared, can scarcely become aware of it, govern its impact, or, if necessary, reject it....

"In both the search for news and in reporting it, there must be full respect for the laws of morality and for the legitimate rights and dignity of the individual. For not all knowledge is helpful, but 'it is charity that edifies....'

"The principal moral responsibility for the proper use of the media of social communication falls on newsmen, writers, actors, designers, producers, displayers, distributors, operators and sellers, as well as critics and all others who play any part in the production and transmission of mass presentations. It is quite evident what gravely important responsibilities they have in the present day when they are in a position to lead the human race to good or to evil by informing or arousing mankind.

"Thus, they must adjust their economic, political or artistic and technical aspects so as never to oppose the common good. For the purpose of better achieving this goal, they are to be commended when they join professional associations, which—even under a code, if necessary, of sound moral practice—oblige their members to show respect for morality in the duties and tasks of their craft.

"They ought always to be mindful, however, that a great many of their readers and audience are young people, who need a press and entertainment that offer them decent amusement and cultural uplift. In addition, they should see to it that communications or presentations concerning religious matters are entrusted to worthy and experienced hands and are carried out with fitting reverence....

"Public authority, which legitimately concerns itself with the health of the citizenry, is obliged, through the promulgation and careful enforcement of laws, to exercise a fitting and careful watch lest grave damage befall public morals and the welfare of society through the base use of these media....

"Special care should be taken to safeguard young people from printed matter and performances which may be harmful at their age."

—DECREE ON MEDIA OF SOCIAL COMMUNICATION

What are the responsibilities of readers, listeners and viewers?

"All who, of their own free choice, make use of these media of communications as readers, viewers or listeners have special obligations. For a proper choice demands that they fully favor those presentations that are outstanding for their moral goodness, their knowledge and their artistic or technical merit. They ought, however, to avoid those that may be a cause or occasion of spiritual harm to themselves, or that can lead others into danger through base example, or that hinder desirable presentations and promote those that are evil. To patronize such presentations, in most instances, would merely reward those who use these media only for profit.

"In order that those who make use of these media may fulfill the moral code, they ought not to neglect to inform themselves in time about judgments passed by authorities competent in these matters. They ought also to follow such judgments according to the norms of an upright conscience. So that they may more easily resist improper inducements and rather encourage those that are desirable, let them take care to guide and instruct their consciences with suitable aids....

"It is quite unbecoming for the Church's children idly to permit the message of salvation to be thwarted or impeded by the technical delays or expenses, however vast, which are encountered by the very nature of these media.

"...The Synod earnestly invites those organizations and individuals who possess financial and technical ability to support these media freely and generously with their resources and their skills, inasmuch as they contribute to genuine culture and the apostolate."

— DECREE ON MEDIA OF SOCIAL COMMUNICATION

CHRISTIANS—SONS OF GOD

"In the beginning was the Word, and the Word was with God and the Word was God. He was in the beginning with God. All things were made through him, and without him was made nothing that has been made. In him was life, and the life was the light of men. And the light shines in the darkness; and the darkness grasped it not.... He came unto his own, and his own received him not. But to as many as received him he gave the power of becoming sons of God; to those who believe in his name: who were not born of blood, nor of the will of flesh, nor of the will of men, but of God. And the Word was made flesh, and dwelt among us. And we saw his glory—glory as of the only-begotten of the Father—full of grace and of truth.... And of his fullness we have all received grace for grace" (John 1:1-16).

CHRIST, OUR MODEL

"Only in the mystery of the incarnate Word does the mystery of man take on light. For Adam, the first man, was a figure of Him who was to come, namely Christ the Lord. Christ, the final Adam, by the revelation of the mystery of the Father and His love, fully reveals man to man himself and makes his supreme calling clear. It is not surprising, then, that in Him all the aforementioned truths find their root and attain their crown.

"He who is 'the image of the invisible God' (Colossians 1:15), is Himself the perfect man. To the sons of Adam He restores the divine likeness which had been disfigured from the first sin onward. Since human nature as He assumed it was not annulled, by that very fact it has been raised up to a divine dignity in our respect too. For by His incarnation the Son of God has united Himself in some fashion with every man. He worked with human hands, He thought with a human mind, acted by human choice and loved with a human heart. Born of the Virgin Mary, He has truly been made one of us, like us in all things except sin.

"As an innocent lamb He merited for us life by the free shedding of His own blood. In Him God reconciled us to Himself and among ourselves; from bondage to the devil and sin He delivered us, so that each one of us can say with the Apostle: The Son of God 'loved me and gave himself up for me' (Galatians 2:20). By suffering for us He not only provided us with an example for our imitation, He blazed a trail, and if we follow it, life and death are made holy and take on a new meaning.

"The Christian man, conformed to the likeness of that Son who is the first-born of many brothers, received 'the first-fruits of the Spirit' (Romans 8:23) by which he becomes capable of discharging the new law of love. Through this Spirit, who is 'the pledge of our inheritance' (Ephesians 1:14), the whole man is renewed from within, even to the achievement of 'the redemption of the body' (Romans 8:23): 'If the Spirit of him who raised Jesus from the dead dwells in you; then he who raised Jesus Christ from the dead will also bring to life your mortal bodies because of his Spirit who dwells in you' (Romans 8:11).

"Pressing upon the Christian to be sure are the need and the duty to battle against evil through manifold tribulations and even to suffer death. But, linked with the paschal mystery and patterned on the dying Christ, he will hasten forward to resurrection in the strength which comes from hope.

"All this holds true not only for Christians, but for all men of good will in whose hearts grace works in an unseen way. For, since Christ died for all men, and since the ultimate vocation of man is in fact one, and divine, we ought to believe that the Holy Spirit in a manner known only to God offers to every man the possibility of being associated with this paschal mystery.

"Such is the mystery of man, and it is a great one, as seen by believers in the light of Christian revelation. Through Christ and in Christ, the riddles of sorrow and death grow meaningful. Apart from His Gospel, they overwhelm us. Christ has risen, destroying death by His death; He has lavished life upon us so that, as sons in the Son, we can cry out in the Spirit: Abba, Father!"

— PASTORAL CONSTITUTION ON CHURCH IN MODERN WORLD

CHRISTIAN HOLINESS

"Jesus, seeing the crowds, went up the mountain. And when he was seated, his disciples came to him. And opening his mouth he taught them, saying:

"Blessed are the poor in spirit, for theirs is the kingdom of heaven.

"Blessed are the meek, for they shall possess the earth.

"Blessed are they who mourn, for they shall be comforted.

"Blessed are they who hunger and thirst for justice, for they shall be satisfied.

"Blessed are the merciful, for they shall obtain mercy.

"Blessed are the clean of heart, for they shall see God.

"Blessed are the peacemakers, for they shall be called children of God.

"Blessed are they who suffer persecution for justice' sake, for theirs is the kingdom of heaven" (Matthew 5:1-11).

CHRIST'S CHURCH—
HUMAN AND DIVINE

It is of the essence of the Church that she be both human and divine, visible and yet invisibly equipped, eager to act and yet intent on contemplation, present in this world and yet not at home in it; and she is all these things in such wise that in her the human is directed and subordinated to the divine, the visible likewise to the invisible, action to contemplation, and this present world to that city yet to come, which we seek.

—*Dogmatic Constitution on Church*

The Church does not see herself as one more human institution in a world of many institutions. She does not view herself as an organization of social service at a time when there are so many such services available to us. The Church is a sacred, religious, charismatic, incarnational reality. The Church is the complement of the Redeemer, while Christ, in a sense, attains through the Church a fullness in all things.

—*U.S. Bishops' Pastoral Letter,*
The Church in Our Day

Did the work of Jesus Christ end with His ascension?

The work of Jesus Christ did not end with His ascension because He gave the Church the mandate to continue it throughout all the centuries and to extend it to all peoples.

In what form did Jesus Christ institute the Church?

Jesus Christ instituted the Church as an hierarchical and monarchical society; He chose twelve apostles whom He formed and sent to preach; He promised to Peter the primacy and to all the apostles the power to rule, to govern, and to sanctify souls; after the resurrection, He conferred on Peter and the apostles certain powers, which they then passed on to their successors.

What is the Church?

The Second Vatican Council (Dogmatic Constitution on the Church, n. 8) described it thus: "Christ, the one Mediator, established and continually sustains here on earth His holy Church, the community of faith, hope and charity, as an entity with visible delineation through which He communicated truth and grace to all.

"This is the one Church of Christ which in the Creed is professed as one, holy, catholic and apostolic, which our Savior, after His resurrection, commissioned Peter to shepherd, and him and the other apostles to extend and direct with authority, which He erected for all ages as 'the pillar and mainstay of the truth.' This Church constituted and organized in the world as a society, subsists in the Catholic Church, which is governed by the successor of Peter and by the bishops in communion with him."

Why did Jesus Christ institute the Church?
Jesus Christ instituted the Church to continue His mission of communicating supernatural life to souls and thus lead them to eternal happiness.

What is the intimate nature of the Church?
In her intimate nature, the Church is a supernatural organism, inasmuch as she constitutes the Mystical Body of Jesus Christ. The invisible Head is Christ Himself; the members are the faithful united to Him by means of grace; the soul is the Holy Spirit who entirely enlightens her, rules her and sanctifies her.

How did Vatican II describe the Holy Spirit's role in the Church?
"When the work which the Father gave the Son to do on earth was accomplished, the Holy Spirit was sent on the day of Pentecost in order that

He might continually sanctify the Church, and thus, all those who believe would have access through Christ in one Spirit to the Father. He is the Spirit of Life, a fountain of water springing up to life eternal. To men, dead in sin, the Father gives life through Him, until, in Christ, He brings to life their mortal bodies. The Spirit dwells in the Church and in the hearts of the faithful, as in a temple. In them He prays on their behalf and bears witness to the fact that they are adopted sons. The Church, which the Spirit guides in the way of all truth and which He unified in communion and in works of ministry, He both equips and directs with hierarchical and charismatic gifts and adorns with His fruits. By the power of the Gospel He makes the Church keep the freshness of youth. Uninterruptedly He renews it and leads it to perfect union with its Spouse. The Spirit and the Bride both say to Jesus, the Lord, 'Come!' "

— DOGMATIC CONSTITUTION ON THE CHURCH

Who are the living members of the Church?
The living members of the Church are of three kinds: the just living on the earth (the pilgrim Church); the souls already saved, but still detained in a place of expiation (the suffering Church); the blessed of heaven (the triumphant Church).

Is the pilgrim Church an entirely supernatural society?
The pilgrim Church is supernatural in her origin, in her constitution, in her means and in her

end. However, as a society living and working on earth, she is made up of men subject to the necessities of life.

How many elements are there in the Church? In the Church there is a divine element always the same and immutable—as for example, doctrine—and a human element which is **changeable** and perfectible—as for example, the methods of teaching and the very members of the Church.

"Those who have searched not alone in books but in the depths of their own soul for what it means to belong to the Church, find and feel this interior response, namely, that belonging to the Church means not only enrollment in a society but likewise participation in a circulation of the supernatural benefits of faith, hope, charity and grace. It means being members of an exterior, visible communion which is produced and sustained by brethren appointed to act as pastors and fathers, in a word, by the hierarchy, and it means being members of an interior communion animated by the Holy Spirit."

—PAUL VI, ADDRESS, NOVEMBER 28, 1964

Can a Christian separate these two elements in practice—that is, can he profess adherence to the divine, charismatic element of the Church while disregarding the institutional or visible element? "Some seek to divide the Church neatly into her institutional and her charismatic components, to declare oversimply what is Gospel and what is grace, what is Church and what is Christ. The premises of such divisions are frequently forced and always over simplified, even when based on appeal to isolated phrases of Scripture. A more reasoned and faithful reading of the sources of theology will discover that, while some elements in the Church are unmistakably spiritual and some manifestly institutional, most, if not all, are blends of the two. Episcopacy and papacy not only represent institution, Gospel, and Church; they are likewise charismatic, supernaturally vital, and signs of Christ.

"Conversely, there is no genuinely charismatic figure who does not have relationship to institution, Gospel and Church. Catholicism glories in the history of its powerfully charismatic and persuasively prophetic persons: its reformers, many of its mystics, its saints among the laity of both sexes, the clergy of every rank, and even its children. But it is not without gratitude to those institutional personalities who, whatever the human defects which characterize even the saints among them and certainly the sinners, historically helped maintain the Church's continuity, stability and organized witness in the world....

"Who fails to recognize how the institutional and charismatic elements of the Church were interwoven and exemplified in the organized assembly of Vatican II, a contemporary reminder that ours is a Church of charisms? Who fails to see how structured and institutionalized was even the charismatic Church of Pentecost? (cf. Acts 1:23-26; 2:42-47)

"There can hardly be a cleavage between Gospel and grace, between Church and Christ, between episcopacy and charism, between priesthood and laity, between apostolicity and the Holy Spirit."   —U.S. BISHOPS' PASTORAL LETTER, CHURCH IN OUR DAY

"Do not separate the Spirit from the hierarchy, from the institutional structure of the Church, as if they were two antagonistic expressions of Christianity, or as if one, the Spirit, could be obtained by us without the ministry of the other, the Church, the qualified instrument of truth and grace. It is true that the Spirit 'blows where it will' (John 3:8). But we cannot presume that He will come to us, if we are deliberately absent from the vehicle, chosen by Christ, to communicate Him to us. He who does not adhere to the Body of Christ—we will repeat with St. Augustine—leaves the sphere animated by the Spirit of Christ."

—POPE PAUL VI, MAY 26, 1971

Why does the Church take an interest even in material things?

The Church is essentially concerned with eternal goods; nevertheless, she intervenes in those things of the temporal order which are essential to her spiritual mission, to her existence and activity, and to the welfare of mankind. Regarding this last point, Vatican II stated: "It is clear that men are not deterred by the Christian message from building up the world, or impelled to neglect the welfare of their fellows, but they are rather more stringently bound to do these very things."

—PASTORAL CONSTITUTION ON CHURCH IN MODERN WORLD

Has the Church, besides eternal goods, brought temporal goods to humanity also?

From her beginning, the Church, besides the eternal goods, has brought to mankind immense temporal goods, in the scientific order, in family and social life, and all the sections of true civilization, continually elevating the tenor of life.

How do atheists view temporal activity?

"Atheism maintains that we are now mature enough to live **autonomously,** that now the destiny of man will depend only on ourselves. Marxist atheism states that faith in God diverts energies from the organization of the earthly city: religion is an opium. This is also the position of Sartre, for example, for whom freedom is at every moment the absolute beginning: there is nothing before me, my freedom is origin, creation, prime cause; everything is possible for me and everything depends absolutely and only on me."

— JEAN CARDINAL DANIELOU, CHRISTIAN FAITH AND TODAY'S MAN

What is secularization?

"Secularization is the idea that we must convince ourselves that the society of tomorrow will have no room for God or for the sacred, and that we will have to resign ourselves to a humanity that is completely and exclusively secular. To accept this idea, as many Christians and many theologians do today, is criminal."

— JEAN CARDINAL DANIELOU, CHRISTIAN FAITH AND TODAY'S MAN

Why is secularization dangerous?

"The world today does not need greater social organization but a Savior: man today needs someone who will answer the fundamental problems of his existence, which no social structure has ever been able to answer. And it would be sheer madness if once again, fifty years behind their times, Christians were to teach a Christianity that was nothing but social humanism, just when the men of today are beginning to discover its deficiencies and once more feel the need of God. It would be a distressing sight to see men ask for God from a Church no longer able to offer Him."

—JEAN CARDINAL DANIELOU, CHRISTIAN FAITH AND TODAY'S MAN

Are we responsible for the future of the world?
"God did not give us a definitively complete world: He gave us, on the contrary, a world to be constructed. Therefore our creativity, our initiative and our responsibilities are immense.

"We are responsible for the future of the world. This does not mean that we alone are responsible and that everything solely depends on us; it depends on God and it depends on us. It depends on us—and therefore our passivity is contrary to the sense of creation—but it also depends on God."

—JEAN CARDINAL DANIELOU, CHRISTIAN FAITH AND TODAY'S MAN

What is the role of the Christian in human society?
"Because of the very economy of salvation the faithful should learn how to distinguish carefully between those rights and duties which are theirs as members of the Church, and those which they have as members of human society. Let them strive to reconcile the two, remembering that in every temporal affair they must be guided by a Christian conscience, since even

in secular business there is no human activity which can be withdrawn from God's dominion. In our own time, however, it is most urgent that this distinction and also this harmony should shine forth more clearly than ever in the lives of the faithful, so that the mission of the Church may correspond more fully to the special conditions of the world today. For it must be admitted that the temporal sphere is governed by its own principles, since it is rightly concerned with the interests of this world. But that ominous doctrine which attempts to build a society with no regard whatever for religion, and which attacks and destroys the religious liberty of its citizens, is rightly to be rejected."

– DOGMATIC CONSTITUTION ON CHURCH

"The Church, at once a visible association and a spiritual community, goes forward together with humanity and experiences the same earthly lot which the world does. She serves as a leaven and as a kind of soul for human society as it is to be renewed in Christ and transformed into God's family."

– PASTORAL CONSTITUTION ON CHURCH IN MODERN WORLD

What are the characteristics of the mission of the Church?

The characteristics of the mission of the Church are: **universality** in regard to time, place, and people; **indefectibility,** even though constantly a victim of persecution; **infallibility** in matters of faith and morals; **visibility,** in such a manner that in every age and in every place she can be recognized by everyone as the true Church of Jesus Christ.

THE "INSTITUTIONAL" CHURCH

"Nothing in the created universe is potentially more sacred than the human: the human person, human gestures, human words. Through these potentially most sacred of visible realities, the Church acquires her visibility. Sacred though these realities may become, they are not immune from the imperfection and sinfulness of the human condition. And so one must not be utopian in what he expects of his fellowmen, even when they are called by the Spirit or sacramentally ordained for the Church of Jesus Christ. But neither may one be pessimistic about God's power and choice to sanctify us through our fellowmen and created signs.

"Of all things visible by which men are drawn to God, the Church is the sum and the sign. And yet, there recurs in history the temptation to take scandal at the idea of God present among men in flesh like their own, or of a Church audible, visible, human as well as divine, and therefore inevitably imperfect. Hence some men turn away impatiently from the Church when they find her less than ideal. This turning away from the Church would be less harmful if there were any beneficent alternative to the Church. History records none.

"Men may criticize the Church but no one can create the indispensable substitute for her. One who lives the life of the Church senses in his heart not only the sentiments expressed by Peter's haunting question, 'Lord, to whom else shall we go?' (John 6:68), but also the conviction that there is no better place to be in than in the Church: 'It is good for us to be here' (Mark 9:5). In other words, the Church brings into history an experience we would not wish to forego even were it possible to do so without harm to ourselves and to our brethren.''

— U.S. BISHOPS' PASTORAL LETTER, CHURCH IN OUR DAY

THE PEOPLE OF GOD

"As God did not create man for life in isolation, but for the formation of social unity, so also 'it has pleased God to make men holy and save them not merely as individuals, without bond or link between them, but by making them into a single people, a people which acknowledges Him in truth and serves Him in holiness.' So from the beginning of salvation history He has chosen men not just as individuals but as members of a certain community. Revealing His mind to them, God called these chosen ones 'His people' (Exodus 3:7-12), and even made a covenant with them on Sinai....

"This communitarian character is developed and consummated in the work of Jesus Christ. For the very Word made flesh willed to share in the human fellowship. He was present at the wedding of Cana, visited the house of Zacchaeus, ate with publicans and sinners. He revealed the love of the Father and the sublime vocation of man in terms of the most common of social realities and by making use of the speech and the imagery of plain everyday life. Willingly obeying the laws of his country, He sanctified those human ties, especially family ones, which are the source of social structures. He chose to lead the life proper to an artisan of His time and place.

"In His preaching He clearly taught the sons of God to treat one another as brothers. In His prayers He pleaded that all His disciples might be as 'one.' Indeed as the redeemer of all, He offered Himself for all even to point of death. 'Greater love than this no one has, that one lay down his life for his friends' (John 15:13). He commanded His apostles to preach to all peoples the Gospel's message that the human race was to become the Family of God, in which the fullness of the Law would be love.

"As the firstborn of many brethren and by the giving of His Spirit, He founded after His death and resurrection a new brotherly community composed of all those who receive Him in faith and in love. This He did through His Body, which is the Church. There everyone, as members one of the other, would render mutual service according to the different gifts bestowed on each.

"This solidarity must be constantly increased until that day on which it will be brought to perfection. Then, saved by grace, men will offer flawless glory to God as a family beloved of God and of Christ their Brother."

—PASTORAL CONSTITUTION ON CHURCH IN MODERN WORLD

THE APOSTLES' CREED

I believe in God, the Father Almighty, Creator of heaven and earth; and in Jesus Christ, His only Son, our Lord; who was conceived by the Holy Spirit, born of the Virgin Mary, suffered under Pontius Pilate, was crucified, died and was buried. He descended into hell; the third day He arose again from the dead; He ascended into heaven, sits at the right hand of God, the Father Almighty; from thence He shall come to judge the living and the dead. I believe in the Holy Spirit, the holy Catholic Church, the communion of saints, the forgiveness of sins, the resurrection of the body and life everlasting. Amen.

HOW IS CHRIST'S CHURCH DISTINGUISHED?

This is the one Church of Christ which in the Creed is professed as one, holy, catholic and apostolic, which our Savior, after His resurrection, commissioned Peter to shepherd, and him and the other apostles to extend and direct with authority, which He erected for all ages as 'the pillar and mainstay of the truth.'
— *Dogmatic Constitution on the Church*

What are the characteristic marks which distinguish the true Church of Jesus Christ?
The characteristic marks which distinguish the true Church of Jesus Christ are especially: unity, holiness, catholicity and apostolicity.

What is meant by the Church's unity?
All members of the true Church of Jesus Christ of all times and of all places had, have and will always have unity of faith, of rule and of liturgical worship, forming thus a sole body, under the leadership of the visible head of the Church, the Roman Pontiff.

In what does the holiness of the Church consist?
The holiness of the Church consists in the very holiness of her invisible Head, Jesus Christ, and of the Holy Spirit, who is her soul. Moreover, her doctrine, morals and sacraments are holy. Her members are all called to holiness and many actually attain it.

In what does the catholicity of the Church consist?
Jesus Christ ordered the Church to gather together all men of all times and of all places: in this consists her catholicity. The Church has always felt the vocation to universality

and in actual fact she has spread to the four corners of the earth.

In what does the apostolicity of the Church consist?

The apostolicity of the Church, of her **origin,** consists in the fact that she is the same society as that of which the apostles were the foundation. The apostolicity **of her doctrine and means of salvation** consists in her divine immutable elements. Her apostolicity of **succession** is the unbroken line of Roman Pontiffs. Where Peter is, or his successor, there is the Church.

What is the significance of the word "Roman" in the title "Roman Catholic Church"?

Peter, head of the Church, came to Rome; there he established his pontificate and there he died; every successor of his is Bishop of Rome and head of the universal Church. The Church can never be separated from her head, the Roman Pontiff. He who lives united to the Pope, lives united to Jesus Christ, as the branch to the vine.

Can he who is outside of the Church save himself?

He who is outside the Church **through his own fault** is not on the way of salvation; he who, instead, is outside of the Church **in good faith** is unknowingly related to her in desire and resolution, and if he lives well, can attain to heaven.

Who are those who depart from the Pope and from Jesus Christ?

They depart from the Pope and from Jesus Christ who refuse them obedience; who deny some truth of faith taught by them; those who fight against them, and those who belong to condemned movements.

How does the Catholic Church compare with other religions?

Because of her truth, holiness, supernaturalness of life, and above all, because she was instituted by God, the Catholic Church is superior to ever other religion.

How does the Church regard Hinduism and Buddhism?

"In Hinduism, men contemplate the divine mystery and express it through an inexhaustible abundance of myths and through searching philosophical inquiry. They seek freedom from the anguish of our human condition either through ascetical practices or profound meditation or a flight to God with love and trust.

"Again, Buddhism, in its various forms, realizes the radical insufficiency of this changeable world; it teaches a way by which men, in a devout and confident spirit, may be able either to acquire the state of perfect liberation, or attain, by their own efforts or through higher help, supreme illumination. . . .

"The Catholic Church rejects nothing that is true and holy in these religions. She regards with sincere reverence those ways of conduct and of life, those precepts and teachings which, though differing in many aspects from the ones she holds and sets forth, nonetheless often reflect a ray of that Truth which enlightens all

Christians invite our
courageous century to attain
the further courage of faith.

They invite a waiting
expectant age, in all its waiting
to await even God.

men. Indeed, she proclaims, and ever must proclaim Christ 'the way, the truth, and the life' (John 14:6), in whom men may find the fullness of religious life, in whom God has reconciled all things to Himself."

— DECLARATION ON RELATION OF CHURCH
TO NON-CHRISTIAN RELIGIONS

In what ways does Christianity surpass these religions?

The ways in which Christianity is superior to these religions are many. In particular it is superior for the miracles with which Jesus Christ proved the divinity of its doctrine; for the excellence of Christian theological and moral doctrine; for its propagation, a true miracle of the moral order.

What common grounds exist between Christians and Moslems?

"The Church regards with esteem also the Moslems. They adore the one God, living and subsisting in Himself, merciful and all-powerful, the Creator of heaven and earth, who has spoken to men; they take pains to submit wholeheartedly to even His inscrutable decrees, just as Abraham, with whom the faith of Islam takes pleasure in linking itself, submitted to God. Though they do not acknowledge Jesus as God, they revere Him as a prophet. They also honor Mary, His virgin Mother; at times they even call on her with devotion. In addition, they await the day of judgment when God will render their deserts to all those who have been raised up from the dead. Finally, they value the moral life and worship God especially through prayer, almsgiving and fasting."

— DECLARATION ON THE RELATION OF CHURCH
TO NON-CHRISTIAN RELIGIONS

What are some points in which Mohammedanism differs from Christianity?

The founder of Mohammedanism did not prove with miracles that special mission he claimed to have; and some of Mohammedanism's teachings are favorable to the passions of lechery and cruelty.

What does the Church teach regarding those of the Jewish faith?

"The Church of Christ acknowledges that, according to God's saving design, the beginnings of her faith and her election are found already among the Patriarchs, Moses and the prophets. She professes that all who believe in Christ— Abraham's sons according to faith—are included in the same Patriarch's call, and likewise that the salvation of the Church is mysteriously foreshadowed by the Chosen People's exodus from the land of bondage.

"The Church, therefore, cannot forget that she received the revelation of the Old Testament through the people with whom God in His inexpressible mercy concluded the Ancient Covenant. Nor can she forget that she draws sustenance from the root of that well-cultivated olive tree onto which have been grafted the wild shoots, the Gentiles. Indeed, the Church believes that by His cross Christ, our Peace, reconciled Jews and Gentiles, making both one in Himself.

"The Church keeps ever in mind the words of the Apostle about his kinsmen: 'theirs is the sonship and the glory and the covenants and the law and the worship and the promises; theirs are the fathers and from them is the Christ according to the flesh' (Romans 9:4-5), the Son of the Virgin Mary. She also recalls that the apostles, the Church's mainstay and pillars, as well as most of the early disciples who proclaimed Christ's Gospel to the world, sprang from the Jewish people.

"As Holy Scripture testifies, Jerusalem did not recognize the time of her visitation, nor did the Jews in large number accept the Gospel; indeed not a few opposed its spreading. Nevertheless, God holds the Jews most dear for the sake of their Fathers; He does not repent of the gifts He makes or of the calls He issues— such is the witness of the Apostle. In company with the prophets and the same Apostle, the Church awaits that day, known to God alone, on which all peoples will address the Lord in a single voice and 'serve him shoulder to shoulder' (Sophonia 3:9)."

—DECLARATION ON RELATION OF CHURCH
TO NON-CHRISTIAN RELIGIONS

What is the relationship between the Church and non-Catholic Christians (Separated Brethren)? "The Church recognizes that in many ways she is linked with those who, being baptized, are honored with the name of Christian, though they do not profess the faith in its entirety or do not preserve unity of communion with the successor of Peter.

"For there are many who honor Sacred Scripture, taking it as a norm of belief and a pattern of life, and who show a sincere zeal. They lovingly believe in God the Father Almighty and in Christ, the Son of God and Savior. They are consecrated by baptism, in which they are united with Christ. They also recognize and accept other sacraments within their own Churches or ecclesiastical communities. Many of them rejoice in the episcopate, celebrate the Holy Eucharist and cultivate devotion toward the Virgin Mother of God. They also share with us in prayer and other spiritual benefits.

"Likewise we can say that in some real way they are joined with us in the Holy Spirit, for to them too He gives His gifts and graces whereby He is operative among them with His sanctifying power. Some indeed He has strengthened to the extent of the shedding of their blood.

"In all of Christ's disciples the Spirit arouses the desire to be peacefully united, in the manner determined by Christ, as one flock under one shepherd, and He prompts them to pursue this end.

"Mother Church never ceases to pray, hope and work that this may come about. She exhorts her children to purification and renewal so that the sign of Christ may shine more brightly over the face of the earth."

— DOGMATIC CONSTITUTION ON CHURCH

THE GOOD SHEPHERD

Jesus said to His disciples: "I am the good shepherd. The good shepherd lays down his life for his sheep. But the hireling, who is not a shepherd, whose own the sheep are not, sees the wolf coming and flees. And the wolf snatches and scatters the sheep; but the hireling flees because he is a hireling, and has no concern for the sheep.

"I am the good shepherd, and I know mine and mine know me, even as the Father knows me and I know the Father; and I lay down my life for my sheep. **And other sheep I have that are not of this fold. Them also I must bring, and they shall hear my voice, and there shall be one fold and one shepherd**" (John 10:11-16).

CATHOLICITY OF THE FAITH

"Sublime and consoling thought for a Catholic!...That same doctrine of peace which Christ preached on the mountain, that same doctrine which Peter announced in Rome, and Paul in Ephesus, and John Chrysostom in Constantinople, and Augustine in Hippo, Ambrose in Milan, and Remigius in France, Boniface in Germany, Patrick in Ireland, Augustine in England, Pelagius in Scotland, is preached now in every Catholic Church in the world, throughout the entire year, from January to December. **Christ yesterday and today, immutable in all ages.**"

— CARDINAL GIBBONS, FAITH OF OUR FATHERS

THE CHURCH AND NON-CHRISTIANS

"In our time, when day by day mankind is being drawn closer together, and the ties between different peoples are becoming stronger, the Church examines more closely her relationship to non-Christian religions. In her task of promoting unity and love among men, indeed among nations, she considers above all in this declaration what men have in common and what draws them to fellowship....

"The Church exhorts her sons, that through dialogue and collaboration with the followers of other religions, carried out with prudence and love and in witness to the Christian faith and life, they recognize, preserve and promote the good things, spiritual and moral, as well as the socio-cultural values found among these men. ...

"We cannot truly call on God, the Father of all, if we refuse to treat in a brotherly way any man, created as he is in the image of God. Man's relation to God the Father and his relation to men his brothers are so linked together that Scripture says: "He who does not love does not know God" (1 John 4:8).

"No foundation therefore remains for any theory or practice that leads to discrimination between man and man or people and people, so far as their human dignity and the rights flowing from it are concerned."

—DECLARATION ON RELATION OF CHURCH
TO NON-CHRISTIAN RELIGIONS

OUR SEPARATED BRETHREN

"Even in the beginnings of this one and only Church of God there arose certain rifts, which the Apostle strongly condemned. But in subsequent centuries much more serious dissensions made their appearance and quite large communities came to be separated from full communion with the Catholic Church—for which, often enough, men of both sides were to blame. The children who are born into these Communities and who grow up believing in Christ cannot be accused of the sin involved in the separation, and the Catholic Church embraces them as brothers, with respect and affection. For men who believe in Christ and have been truly baptized are in communion with the Catholic Church even though this communion is imperfect.

"The differences that exist in varying degrees between them and the Catholic Church—whether in doctrine and sometimes in discipline, or concerning the structure of the Church—do indeed create many obstacles, sometimes serious ones, to full ecclesiastical communion. The ecumenical movement is striving to overcome these obstacles. But even in spite of them it remains true that all who have been justified by faith in Baptism are members of Christ's body, and have a right to be called Christian, and so are correctly accepted as brothers by the children of the Catholic Church.

"Moreover, some and even very many of the significant elements and endowments which together go to build up and give life to the Church itself, can exist outside the visible boundaries of the Catholic Church: the written word of God; the life of grace; faith, hope and charity, with the other interior gifts of the Holy Spirit, and visible elements too. All of these, which come from Christ and lead back to Christ, belong by right to the one Church of Christ.

"The brethren divided from us also use many liturgical actions of the Christian religion. These most certainly can truly engender a life of grace in ways that vary according to the condition of each Church or Community. These liturgical actions must be regarded as capable of giving access to the community of salvation.

"It follows that the separated Churches and Communities as such, though we believe them to be deficient in some respects, have been by no means deprived of significance and importance in the mystery of salvation. For the Spirit of Christ has not refrained from using them as means of salvation which derive their efficacy from the very fullness of grace and truth entrusted to the Church.

"Nevertheless, our separated brethren, whether considered as individuals or as Communities and Churches, are not blessed with that unity which Jesus Christ wished to bestow on all those who through Him were born again into one body, and with Him quickened to newness of life—that unity which the Holy Scriptures and the ancient Tradition of the Church proclaim.

"For it is only through Christ's Catholic Church, which is 'the all-embracing means of salvation,' that they can benefit fully from the means of salvation. We believe that our Lord entrusted all the blessings of the New Covenant to the apostolic college alone, of which Peter is the head, in order to establish the one body of Christ on earth to which all should be fully incorporated who belong in any way to the People of God.

"This People of God, though still in its members liable to sin, is ever growing in Christ during its pilgrimage on earth, and is guided by God's gentle wisdom, according to His hidden designs, until it shall happily arrive at the fullness of eternal glory in the heavenly Jerusalem."   — DECREE ON ECUMENISM

THE CHURCH, TEACHER OF TRUTH

When He had by His death and His resurrection completed once for all in Himself the mysteries of our salvation and the renewal of all things, the Lord, having now received all power in heaven and on earth (cf. Matthew 28:18), before He was taken up into heaven (cf. Acts of the Apostles 1:11), founded His Church as the sacrament of salvation and sent His apostles into all the world just as He Himself had been sent by His Father (cf. John 20:21), commanding them: "Go, therefore, and make disciples of all nations, baptizing them in the name of the Father and of the Son and of the Holy Spirit; teaching them to observe all that I have commanded you" (Matthew 28:19 ff.) "Go into the whole world, preach the Gospel to every creature. He who believes and is baptized shall be saved; but he who does not believe, shall be condemned" (Mark 16:15 ff.) Whence the duty that lies on the Church of spreading the faith and the salvation of Christ, not only in virtue of the express command which was inherited from the apostles by the order of bishops, assisted by the priests, together with the successor of Peter and supreme shepherd of the Church, but also in virtue of that life which flows from Christ into His members.

—Decree on the Mission Activity of the Church

However necessary the function of theologians, it is not to the learned that God has confided the duty of authentically interpreting the faith of the Church: that faith is borne by the life of the people whose bishops are responsible for them before God. It is for the bishops to tell the people what God asks them to believe."

—Paul VI, Apostolic Exhortation on the Fifth Anniversary of the Closing of Vatican II

What mandate did the Church receive from Jesus Christ?
The Church received from Jesus Christ the mandate of being, for all mankind, the teacher of truth, of sanctity and of prayer.

Why is the Church the teacher of truth?
The Church is the teacher of truth:

1) because she has received the divine mandate to preach and to propagate the doctrine of Jesus Christ;

2) because Jesus Christ has promised to be continually with her and that the gates of hell shall not prevail against her;

3) because the soul of the Church is the Holy Spirit who, according to the promise of Jesus Christ, "will teach all things; he is the Spirit of truth who teaches all the truth" (John 14:26; 16:13);

4) because Jesus Christ absolutely requires everyone to believe and he who does not believe will be condemned—but how could He condemn us if the Church could teach error?

5) because the apostles and their successors always had knowledge and certainty of the

infallibility of the Church, and the miracles worked by the apostles and by the saints united to the Church point to the intervention of God and confirm the truth taught by them;

6) because the necessity of this living, infallible and perpetual magisterium springs from the very nature of Revelation.

Is "truth" one, or is there a plurality of truths?

"The Catholic Church clearly knows and maintains that there is but one truth, and consequently that contrary 'truths' cannot exist. She declares and bears witness to the saying of the Apostle of the Gentiles, 'The powers we have are used in support of the truth, not against it' (2 Corinthians 13:8).

"The Catholic Church ordains that all that has been divinely revealed must be firmly and faithfully believed; that is, what is contained in the Scriptures, or in oral or written Tradition, and, from the time of the apostles in the course of the centuries, has been approved and defined by the Supreme Pontiffs and the lawful ecumenical councils. Whenever anyone has left this path, the Church using her maternal authority has never ceased to invite him back, again and again, to the right path."

—JOHN XXIII, ENCYCLICAL, NEAR CHAIR OF PETER

In expressing dogmas in contemporary terms, what must be avoided?

"There is a great temptation in religious life today, and in Catholic religious life, to undermine the reverence due to the Church's magisterium and dogmatic commitment to the theological doctrine which it entails. There is an effort to change the textual form in which it is expressed and to change the meaning of its terms, so as to weaken the objective meaning of doctrine, and even sometimes to nullify it. There is consequently a desire to replace it by interpretations, erudite perhaps, but arbitrary and in line with the currents of modern cultural opinion; but they are not always aimed at safeguarding the unequivocal and authentic meaning of Revelation, interpreted by the Church and authoritatively taught by her.''

—PAUL VI, APRIL, 1970

Can there be a "development of doctrine"?

"There will always be development of doctrine as long as man is man, given a mind that is the image of the all-knowing mind of God. But there are also fundamentals of doctrine,... and these must be transmitted undiluted to our children so that they may be prepared to judge, in their later years, what is a development and what is a contradiction of Christian doctrine.''

—JOHN CARDINAL CARBERRY, NEED
FOR ORTHODOX CATHOLIC TEACHING

Can the de-emphasis of certain dogmas be dangerous?

"Many a heresy has been started by emphasizing a few doctrines of the Church, to the exclusion of others equally true and essential.''

—CARDINAL NEWMAN

What is religious assent?

"Religious assent is not passivity but a positive consequence of discipleship in Christ. This assent is required of all of us, bishops and clergy as well as laity, when a doctrine is solemnly and publicly defined by the Bishop of Rome or the episcopal college together with the Pope. It is required of us, furthermore, though not definitively, in that ordinary teaching of the everyday Church which underlies our common faith and action. A Catholic abides not only by the extraordinary decisions of the Church but by its ordinary life as well where faith and discipline are concerned."

— U. S. BISHOPS' PASTORAL, CHURCH IN OUR DAY

What is the function of conscience?

"God does not speak directly and immediately to everyone and in an infallible form. That would give rise to personal interpretations and judgments, to subjectivism and finally to error.

"God manifests His law to each of us through reason, illuminated by faith, as the magisterium of the Church teaches us. Therefore, it is the duty of conscience to know this teaching and to make its own judgment and behavior conform to it. Only in this way does it answer God's voice.

"The magisterium does not take the place of conscience: it illuminates it, forms it and perfects it. To act according to an upright conscience is to make one's personal judgment conform to the magisterium of the Church and not to claim to adapt the latter to one's own wishes.

"Anyone who sincerely seeks the teaching of the Church will find it easily, since it is spread rapidly and amply today. Once it is known, it is necessary to accept it docilely and put it into practice loyally, without interpretations, subterfuges or reservations, without looking for a way to defend one's own judgment and do what is most agreeable for us, eluding the commands of the law."

— ARCHBISHOP COVARRUBIAS, VALPARAISO, CHILE

Does a person commit a fault if he acts with an erroneous conscience?

"Only one who, in spite of his efforts, does not succeed in getting to know this teaching does not commit a fault if he acts according to conscience, even though erroneously. This, however, does not authorize anyone to imitate him. Only error through no fault of one's own or absolute ignorance do not entail sin, but they do not change the law."

— ARCHBISHOP COVARRUBIAS, VALPARAISO, CHILE

What follows from this doctrine of the Church as teacher of truth?

From the infallibility of the ecclesiastical magisterium follows the passive infallibility of the members of the Church; so that all the faithful are certain of possessing the complete truth and of not being deceived or mistaken while they sincerely adhere to the Church. The apostolate of the laity also possesses inerrancy if it participates in and is united to the hierarchical apostolate.

REVELATION AND THE TEACHING CHURCH

"Sacred Tradition and Sacred Scripture form one sacred deposit of the word of God, committed to the Church. Holding fast to this deposit the entire holy people united with their shepherds remain always steadfast in the teaching of the apostles, in the common life, in the breaking of the bread and in prayers, so that holding to, practicing and professing the heritage of the faith, it becomes on the part of the bishops and faithful a single common effort.

"But the task of authentically interpreting the word of God, whether written or handed on, has been entrusted exclusively to the living teaching office of the Church, whose authority is exercised in the name of Jesus Christ. This teaching office is not above the word of God, but serves it, teaching only what has been handed on, listening to it devoutly, guarding it scrupulously and explaining it faithfully in accord with a divine commission and, with the help of the Holy Spirit, it draws from this one deposit of faith everything which it presents for belief as divinely revealed.

"It is clear, therefore, that Sacred Tradition, Sacred Scripture and the teaching authority of the Church, in accord with God's most wise design, are so linked and joined together that one cannot stand without the others, and that all together and each in its own way under the action of the one Holy Spirit contribute effectively to the salvation of souls."

—DOGMATIC CONSTITUTION ON DIVINE REVELATION

THE DANGER OF RELIGIOUS INDIFFERENCE

"There are those who, though they do not deliberately attack the truth, yet, by neglect and extreme carelessness, work against it—as if God has not given us a mind to search for and arrive at the truth. This depraved manner of acting leads by an easy path to this ridiculous opinion: There is no difference between the true and the false, and so all religions are equally true. To use the words of our predecessor, 'this kind of reasoning was aimed at the destruction of all religions, and particularly of the Catholic, which, since it alone is true, cannot, without serious injustice, be placed on a level with the others.'

"Moreover, to reckon that there is no difference between contraries and opposites has surely this ruinous result, that there is no readiness to accept any religion either in theory or in practice. For how can God, who is Truth, approve or tolerate the heedlessness, neglect and indolence of those who, when it is a question of matters affecting the eternal salvation of us all, give no attention at all to the search for and the grasp of the essential truth, nor indeed to paying the lawful worship due to God alone?

"If so much labor and care is expended today in the learning and mastery of human knowledge so that our generation boasts—and with perfect right—of the marvelous progress made in the field of scientific research, why do we not expend equal, or greater industry, skill and ingenuity in assimilating by some sure and safe method, doctrines which affect not earthly and mortal life, but the life in heaven which will have no end?

"Then only, when we have reached the truth which has its source in the Gospel, and which must be introduced into life's activities, then only, we say, will our minds find rest in peace and joy. This joy will far and away exceed that satisfaction which can arise from investigation into human affairs and from these wonderful inventions which we use today and which are daily extolled to the skies."

—POPE JOHN XXIII, ENCYCLICAL, NEAR THE CHAIR OF PETER

THE CHURCH, TEACHER OF HOLINESS

Love for God and neighbor is the first and greatest commandment. Sacred Scripture...teaches us that the love of God cannot be separated from love of neighbor: "If there is any other commandment, it is summed up in this saying: Thou shalt love thy neighbor as thyself...love therefore is the fulfillment of the Law" (Romans 13:9-10; cf. 1 John 4:20). To men growing daily more dependent on one another, and to a world becoming more unified every day, this truth proves to be of paramount importance.

—Pastoral Constitution on Church
in Modern World

161

Why is the Church the teacher of morals and of holiness?
The Church is the teacher of morals and holiness because she has the office of guarding, interpreting, setting forth, and applying in an infallible manner the moral teachings given by Jesus Christ and contained in the Gospel; furthermore she has the mandate to govern and direct souls on the way to sanctity.

What sort of life is a member of the Church to live?
"How are we to live? Taking life as it comes, without thinking about it? Are we to conform passively to the environment, customs, fashions, laws, necessities that happen to surround us, or are we to react somehow, that is, act with a criterion of our own, with a certain freedom, at least of judgment and, where possible, of choice?

"Are we content to be impersonal and mediocre, and perhaps also full of shortcomings, dishonest and bad, or are we to impose a rule, a law on ourselves? Are we to demand of ourselves a style of life, a moral

God gave us a world
to be constructed.
Therefore our creativity,
our initiative and
our responsibilities
are immense.

Jean Cardinal Danielou

discipline, perfection, or can we live without scruples, in the easiest, most pleasant way? And if love is the essential qualification of moral life, how are we to understand it, as an affirmation of selfishness, or as a profession of altruism?

"In His Gospel Christ teaches us by word and example how we must live. And with the inner help of His Spirit, grace, and the exterior assistance of His community, the Church, He makes it possible for us to carry out His bidding.

"Let no one delude himself. Christ is demanding. Christ's life is the narrow way (cf. Matthew 7:14). To be worthy of Him, we must take up our cross (cf. Matthew 10:38). It is not enough to be religious, it is necessary to carry out the divine will in actual fact (Matthew 7:21).

—PAUL VI, MARCH, 1970

Are there norms which will assist us in this task?

"Let no one take fright. For the perfection to which we are called by our Christian election does not complicate and aggravate life, even if it requires us to observe many practical norms, calculated rather to help our faithfulness than to make it more difficult. Christian perfection demands from us above all an inquiry into the fundamental principles of our human being. Our duty seeks to equate itself with our being. We should be what we are. This is the principle of the natural law, about which there is so much discussion today.

"We have all, moreover, sufficient knowledge of this law, the most important precepts of which we find enunciated in the Ten Commandments. And obedience to this law makes us men and Christians.

"In the present-day confusion of the notion of good and evil, licit and illicit, just and unjust, and in the demoralizing spread of crime and immorality, we will do well to preserve and deepen the sense of natural law, that is, of justice, of integrity and of the good, that upright reason inspires continually within our consciences."   —PAUL VI, MARCH, 1970

What are the commandments of God and the precepts of the Church?

The commandments of God are these ten:

"I am the Lord your God:
  1. You shall not have strange gods before me.
  2. You shall not take the name of the Lord your God in vain.
  3. Remember to keep holy the Lord's day.
  4. Honor your father and your mother.
  5. You shall not kill.
  6. You shall not commit adultery.
  7. You shall not steal.
  8. You shall not bear false witness against your neighbor.
  9. You shall not covet your neighbor's wife.
  10. You shall not covet your neighbor's goods.

—EXODUS 20:1-17

The precepts of the Church are these six:

1. To assist at Mass on all Sundays and holydays of obligation.
2. To fast and abstain on the days appointed.
3. To confess our sins at least once a year.
4. To receive Holy Communion during the Easter time.
5. To contribute to the support of the Church.
6. To observe the laws of the Church concerning marriage.

What does the first commandment oblige us to do?
The first commandment obliges us to adore God and God alone, and to love Him above all things.

To adore God is to render Him that worship which we owe Him as the Creator and sovereign Lord of all things.

By the worship owed to God we mean all those acts with which we must honor God and give Him proof of our love.

"And Jesus answered and said to him, 'It is written, The Lord your God shall you worship, and him only shall you serve" (Luke 4:8).

Is it enough to worship God in our hearts?
To God we must render both interior worship and exterior worship.

Interior worship consists in the submission of one's mind, heart and will, with internal acts of faith, hope and charity.

Exterior worship consists in the exterior manifestation of our internal sentiments. Exterior worship includes public worship, and it is made in the name of the Church by persons legitimately delegated, namely, priests, and in the prescribed manner. The principal act of public worship is the celebration of Holy Mass. Regarding our role at Mass Vatican II stated:

"The Church earnestly desires that Christ's faithful, when present at this mystery of faith, should not be there as strangers or silent spectators; on the contrary, through a good understanding of the rites and prayers they should take part in the sacred action conscious of what they are doing, with devotion and full collaboration. They should be instructed by God's word and be nourished at the table of the Lord's body; they should give thanks to God; by offering the Immaculate Victim, not only through the hands of the priest, but also with him, they should learn also to offer themselves; through Christ the Mediator, they should be drawn day by day into ever more perfect union with God and with each other, so that finally God may be all in all." — CONSTITUTION ON SACRED LITURGY

What of devotion to the Sacred Heart?
We must adore our Lord Jesus Christ, because He is God.

The devotion to the Sacred Heart consists in honoring the infinite love of Jesus Christ for men under the symbol of His heart of flesh.

What of devotion to the Blessed Virgin and the saints?
We owe a particular devotion to the Most Blessed Virgin because she is the Mother of

God. Devotion to the Most Blessed Virgin consists in loving her with a filial love, in praying to her with confidence and in imitating her virtues.

It is also our duty to honor the saints, to imitate them in their virtue and to render them a public veneration because they are the friends of God and our protectors from heaven. "Raised up to perfection by the manifold grace of God, and already in possession of eternal salvation, they sing God's perfect praise in heaven and offer prayers for us. By celebrating the passage of these saints from earth to heaven the Church proclaims the paschal mystery achieved in the saints who have suffered and been glorified with Christ; she proposes them to the faithful as examples drawing all to the Father through Christ, and through their merits she pleads for God's favors."

—CONSTITUTION ON SACRED LITURGY

Which virtues make a man a Christian?

Three supernatural virtues are required to form a Christian: faith, hope, and charity.

What is faith?

St. Paul says: "Faith is the substance of things to be hoped for, the evidence of things that are not seen." We believe all that God has revealed, on His word revealing it.

Faith is the first and fundamental virtue, the beginning of Christian life. St. Paul taught that without faith it is impossible to be pleasing to God. We must believe in order to approach God.

In fact, Christ's teaching is very clear: "He who does not believe is already judged."

Faith was the first grace infused in our hearts by God, through Baptism. Faith is a great grace which uplifts or encourages us during our exile, during the dark moments in this world. It is a comfort and a light both for the learned and unlearned.

How is faith lived?

First, by avoiding the dangers to it, such as the company of wrongdoers, the reading of bad literature, pride of mind and of heart. The things of God will remain hidden from the proud and will be made known to the humble.

Second, by showing faith in good actions and not letting human respect interfere. Faith, without good works, is dead; it is like that of the demons who believe and tremble.

He who professes Christ before mankind will be acknowledged by Him before His Father.

What is hope?

Christian hope is the second supernatural virtue which, along with faith, was infused in our heart by the Holy Spirit at Baptism. Through hope we look to God our Father to give us heaven and all the graces needed to attain it.

On what is our hope founded?

Our hope is founded on the merits of our Savior Jesus Christ. Through His death we were reconciled with God, moreover, we have His promise to reward those who serve Him faithfully.

Scripture assures us: "We are the sons of God. But if we are sons, we are heirs also: heirs indeed of God and joint heirs with Christ, provided, however, we suffer with him that we may also be glorified with him" (Romans 8:17).

Well-founded hope avoids the sins of presumption and despair, trusting in God's mercy and not too much in oneself, and never despairing of eternal salvation.

Is hope a source of happiness?

Because of his firm hope, the apostle Paul could declare: "I overflow with joy in all our troubles" (1 Cor 7:4). Hope brings comfort and serenity amid all sorrows, lifting our thoughts to the better life that awaits us.

What is charity?

Charity is friendship, kindness, love for God and others. Love of God and neighbor are two rays of the same flame.

Charity is all-important, the queen of virtues: "If I should speak with the tongues of men and of angels, but do not have charity, I have become as sounding brass or a tinkling cymbal. And if I have prophecy and know all mysteries and all knowledge, and if I have all faith so as to remove mountains, yet do not have charity, I am nothing. And if I distribute all my goods to feed the poor, and if I deliver my body to be burned, yet do not have charity, it profits me nothing." Charity is infused in our hearts by virtue of the Holy Spirit and grows steadily throughout the life of the fervent Christian.

How do we grow in God's friendship?

Love of God grows stronger with every effort to avoid sin, with frequent acts of love for Him, with fervent reception of Holy Communion and the other sacraments, with the practice of virtue, with meditation on the sacred.

How is genuine love of God to be recognized?

Its unmistakable sign is love of neighbor. "By this," said Christ our Divine Master, "will they know that you are my disciples: that you have love for one another."

Love of others must include concern for both their spiritual and temporal welfare.

The spiritual works of mercy are: counsel the doubtful, instruct the ignorant, admonish the sinner, comfort the sorrowful, forgive injuries, bear wrongs patiently, pray for the living and the dead.

The corporal works of mercy are: feed the hungry, give drink to the thirsty, clothe the naked, shelter the homeless, visit the sick, visit the imprisoned, and bury the dead.

God considers as done to Himself what we do to others, be it good or evil.

What does the second commandment require of us?

The second commandment orders us to respect the name of God and hence prohibits the taking of false and rash oaths, cursing, and the breaking of vows either in word or in deed.

"You shall not swear falsely by my name, nor profane the name of your God" (Leviticus 19:12).

What is an oath?
An oath is the calling on God to witness the truth of what we say or promise.

What is blasphemy?
Blasphemy is the use of insulting language against God, religion, the Blessed Virgin and the saints. It is the pronouncement of the holy name of God with hatred or with contempt.

What is a vow?
A vow is a free and deliberate promise made to God by which a person binds himself under pain of sin to do something that is especially pleasing to God.

Is it good to make vows?
It is good to make vows, but only after having thought it over well and having asked the advice of a prudent spiritual director.

"When you have made a vow to the Lord your God, you shall not delay to pay it: because the Lord your God will require it" (Deuteronomy 23:21).

What are we commanded by the third commandment of God?
The third commandment of God commands us to keep holy the Lord's Day.

Are the faithful obliged to assist at Mass on Sundays?
"The Catholic Church has decreed for many centuries that Christians observe a day of rest on Sunday, and that they be present on the same day at the Eucharistic Sacrifice because it renews the memory of the divine redemption

and at the same time imparts its fruits to the souls of men."

—JOHN XXIII, ENCYCLICAL, MATER ET MAGISTRA

"Where permission has been granted by the Apostolic See to fulfill the Sunday obligation on the preceding Saturday evening, pastors should explain the meaning of this permission carefully to the faithful and should ensure that the significance of Sunday is not thereby obscured. The purpose of this concession is in fact to enable the Christians of today to celebrate more easily the day of the resurrection of the Lord."

—INSTRUCTION ON WORSHIP OF EUCHARISTIC MYSTERY

Are the faithful obliged to abstain from activities on Sundays?

The works forbidden on Sundays and holydays are all so-called servile works, that is, manual labor in all fields, unless justified by necessity and charity.

Gain, or the desire to have money for luxuries, is not a legitimate and grave reason. However, a real necessity imposed by an urgent good, either personal or public, is legitimate.

What activities are especially suitable for Sundays and holydays?

Especially suitable are activities that contribute to the good of the spirit, such as religious reading and works of charity, as well as wholesome, relaxing amusements.

What does the fourth commandment oblige us to do?

The fourth commandment orders us to love our parents and superiors, to respect and obey them, and to help them in all their needs. "Children, obey your parents in the Lord, for that is right. 'Honor your father and your mother'—such is the first commandment with a promise—'that it may be well with you, and that you may be long-lived upon the earth'" (Ephesians 6:1-3).

How does one sin against the fourth commandment?

One sins against the love due to parents or lawful superiors when he nurtures hatred and aversion toward them.

One is disrespectful towards them when he answers back, scorns them or maltreats them.

One is disobedient when he does not do as he is told or does so with spitefulness and complaints.

One does not fulfill his duty of helping his parents when he abandons them in poverty, old age or sickness, or when he fails to obtain religious assistance for them.

What are the duties of parents toward their children?

Parents must have their children baptized as soon as possible, raise them, instruct them and give them a Christian education, correct their defects, give them good examples, and help them obtain a suitable position in life.

"Let the father of the family take the place of God among his children, and not only by his authority but by the upright example of his life also stand clearly in the first place.

"Let the mother, however, rule firmly and agreeably over her children by gentleness and virtue in the domestic setting. Let her behave with indulgence and love towards her husband, and along with him, let her carefully instruct and train her family, the most precious gift given by God, to live an upright and religious life."

— JOHN XXIII, ENCYCLICAL, NEAR THE CHAIR OF PETER

What are the duties of a citizen towards his country?

The principal duties of a citizen are: To respect civil authority and obey just laws, that is, conscientiously fulfill all civil duties. The principal civil duties are: to pay taxes; to defend one's country, even at the cost of one's life; to fulfill one's duty of voting.

Is the obligation of bearing arms in the service of one's country binding upon all?

"It seems right that laws make humane provisions for the case of those who for reasons of conscience refuse to bear arms, provided however that they agree to serve the human community in some other way."

— PASTORAL CONSTITUTION ON CHURCH IN MODERN WORLD

What are the duties of a member of the Church with regard to voting?

One's vote must be given to people whose beliefs and programs are sincerely beneficial to everyone. Only from such public servants can we expect just reform, real reconstruction, true welfare. We cannot expect wise and beneficent laws from lawgivers who are enemies of God or atheists.

It is a sin to vote for an enemy of religion, of the nation or of the public well-being, because by voting for him, one voluntarily participates in the evil which such a person could do if he were elected.

It is also a sin not to vote, if, by not voting, one could be the cause of an incapable or perverse candidate being elected.

Consequently, every citizen must not only vote, but he must use this electoral right well and give his vote to conscientious and morally upright candidates.

How patriotic should a Christian be?

"Citizens must cultivate a generous and loyal spirit of patriotism, but without being narrow-minded. This means that they will always direct their attention to the good of the whole human family, united by the different ties which bind together races, peoples and nations."

—PASTORAL CONSTITUTION ON CHURCH IN MODERN WORLD

What does the fifth commandment forbid?

The fifth commandment of God forbids everything that can harm the life of the body or of the soul.

One can injure his neighbor's body by voluntarily causing his death or wounding or beating him unjustly.

One can injure his neighbor's soul with scandal, that is, by causing him to sin. Scandal may be given by words, conversations, writings or examples.

"The works of the flesh are manifest, which are...enmities, contentions...anger, quarrels ...murders, drunkenness, carousings, and suchlike. And concerning these I warn you, as I have warned you, that they who do such things will not attain the kingdom of God" (Galatians 5:19-21).

What are some of the chief crimes committed against human life and dignity?

"Whatever is opposed to life itself, such as any type of **murder, genocide, abortion, euthanasia** or **willful self-destruction,** whatever violates the integrity of the human person, such as mutilation, torments inflicted on body or mind, attempts to coerce the will itself; whatever insults human dignity, such as subhuman living conditions, arbitrary imprisonment, deportation, slavery, prostitution, the selling of women and children; as well as disgraceful working conditions, where men are treated as mere tools for profit, rather than as free and responsible persons; all these things and others of their like are infamies indeed. They poison human society, but they do more harm to those who practice them than those who suffer from the injury. Moreover, they are a supreme dishonor to the Creator.

"...God, the Lord of life, has conferred on men the surpassing ministry of safeguarding life—a ministry which must be fulfilled in a manner which is worthy of man. Therefore from the moment of its conception life must be guarded with the greatest care, while abortion and infanticide are unspeakable crimes."

—PASTORAL CONSTITUTION ON CHURCH IN MODERN WORLD

What does the fifth commandment forbid besides physical injury and scandal?

The fifth commandment also forbids fighting, anger, hatred, revenge, drunkenness and the taking of harmful or dangerous drugs.

Is scandal widespread today?

Scandal is diffused in theaters and in motion picture houses; on the beaches and at resorts; with books and magazines; with television and radio; and with immodest styles. Woe to those who make themselves propagators of scandal!

What are we commanded by the fifth commandment?

The fifth commandment requires us to take care of our own well-being—of both soul and body—and that of our neighbor.

What sins are forbidden by the sixth and ninth commandments?

The sixth commandment of God forbids impure acts, that is, the illegitimate pleasures of the senses, and everything that leads to impurity: looks, literature or shows, words or actions.

The ninth commandment forbids impure thoughts sought or entertained with pleasure: impure imaginings voluntarily excited or not rejected, and evil desires.

"Do you not know that your members are the temples of the Holy Spirit, who is in you, whom you have from God, and that you are not your own? For you have been bought at a great price. Glorify God and bear him in your body" (1 Corinthians 6:19-20).

Is married love noble?

"This love is an eminently human one since it is directed from one person to another through an affection of the will; it involves the good of the whole person, and therefore can enrich the expressions of body and mind with a unique dignity, ennobling these expressions as special ingredients and signs of the friendship distinctive of marriage.

"This love is uniquely expressed and perfected through the marital act. The actions within marriage by which the couple are united intimately and chastely are noble and worthy ones. Expressed in a manner which is truly human, these actions promote that mutual self-giving by which spouses enrich each other with a joyful and a ready will."

—PASTORAL CONSTITUTION ON CHURCH IN MODERN WORLD

What is the true image of married love?

"Sealed by mutual faithfulness and hallowed above all by Christ's sacrament, this love remains steadfastly true in body and in mind, in bright days or dark. It will never be profaned by adultery or divorce. Firmly established by the Lord, the unity of marriage will radiate from the equal personal dignity of wife and husband, a dignity acknowledged by mutual and total love.

"The constant fulfillment of the duties of this Christian vocation demands notable virtue. For this reason, strengthened by grace for holiness of life, the couple will painstakingly cultivate and pray for steadiness of love, large-heartedness and the spirit of sacrifice."

—PASTORAL CONSTITUTION ON CHURCH IN MODERN WORLD

Is the true image of marriage often obscured?

"The excellence of this institution is not every-where reflected with equal brilliance, since polygamy, the plague of divorce, so-called free love and other disfigurements have an obscuring effect. In addition, married love is too often profaned by excessive self-love, the worship of pleasure and illicit practices against human generation."

—PASTORAL CONSTITUTION ON CHURCH IN MODERN WORLD

What does the encyclical "Humanae vitae" teach regarding birth control?

"The encyclical is a positive statement concerning the nature of conjugal love and responsible parenthood, a statement which derives from a global vision of man, an integral view of marriage, and the first principles, at least, of a sound sexuality. It is an obligatory statement, consistent with moral convictions rooted in the traditions of Eastern and Western Christian faith; it is an authoritative statement solemnly interpreting imperatives which are **divine rather than ecclesiastical** in origin. It presents without ambiguity, doubt or hesitation the authentic teaching of the Church concerning the objective evil of that contraception which closes the marital act to the transmission of life, deliberately making it unfruitful. United in collegial solidarity with the Successor of Peter, we proclaim this doctrine."

—U.S. BISHOPS' PASTORAL LETTER, HUMAN LIFE IN OUR DAY

What of pre-marital sex relations?
Pre-marital sex relations are a serious violation of the law of God. Breaking God's law before marriage is no way to draw down His blessings on the marriage. How could one ever hope for chastity and marital fidelity from a young person who could never control himself and master his passions?

What are the consequences of sins of impurity?
As a sin, impurity offends God and causes the loss of grace.

Other sad consequences are blindness of the mind and weakening of the will. He who lives like the animals permits himself to be dragged along only by the low instincts; reason no longer appreciates truth, the intelligence can no longer elevate itself and the will is carried away. Even the heart becomes hardened to the point of no longer feeling remorse. In such conditions it is easy to lose one's faith.

Doctors affirm and experience confirms that this vice greatly injures one's health too. Weakness, weariness and discouragement result.

Even society is devastated. Corrupt people might know how to rise to passing triumphs, but a fatal ruin awaits them. Corruption has always been the only or the principal cause of the downfall of peoples. Immorality is like a rust that inexorably consumes.

What are the principal means for practicing purity?

The principal means for practicing this virtue are frequent Holy Communion and a great devotion to the Blessed Virgin.

In order to preserve oneself from impurity, one must also watch himself and avoid, as much as possible, all dangerous occasions.

What does the seventh commandment forbid?

The seventh commandment of God forbids us to damage our neighbor's property, to unjustly take or keep that which belongs to our neighbor or cause any damage to his goods.

"The beginning of a good way is to do justice; and this is more acceptable with God than to offer sacrifices" (Proverbs 16:5).

To whom do the goods of the earth belong?

All the goods of the earth belong first to God who has created them, and then to those who legitimately possess them.

What purpose should earthly goods serve?

The goods of the earth must serve, according to the will of God, for the good of those who possess them and for the good of others. "Everyone must consider his every neighbor without exception as another self, taking into account first of all his life and the means necessary to living it with dignity, so as not to imitate the rich man who had no concern for the poor man Lazarus."

—PASTORAL CONSTITUTION ON CHURCH IN MODERN WORLD

Who sins against the seventh commandment?
1) Those who unjustly take the goods of others: thieves, usurers, deceivers, employers who do not pay just wages, dishonest workers and all those who deprive someone of that which is due him.

2) Those who unjustly keep the goods of others: debtors who do not pay, thieves who do not return that which they have stolen, and those who do not give back what was entrusted to them.

Are those who transgress this commandment obliged to do more than repent of their sin?
They are obliged to return the things taken or repair the damage done as soon as possible.

What constitutes truly human conditions which ought to be promoted?
In his encyclical "Development of Peoples," Pope Paul VI describes them thus: "the passage from misery towards the possession of necessities, victory over social scourges, the growth of knowledge, the acquisition of culture. Additional conditions that are more human: increased esteem for the dignity of others, the turning toward the spirit of poverty, cooperation for the common good, the will and desire for peace. Conditions that are still more human: the acknowledgment by man of supreme values, and of God their source and their finality.

Conditions that, finally and above all, are more human: faith, a gift of God accepted by the good will of man, and unity in the charity of Christ, who calls us all to share as sons in the life of the living God, the Father of all men."

What are we forbidden by the tenth commandment?

The tenth commandment forbids us even the desire to take or to keep unjustly what belongs to others.

What does the eighth commandment forbid?

The eighth commandment of God forbids: the bearing of false witness in court, lying, the harming of someone's good name.

"Put away lying and speak truth each one with his neighbor, because we are members of one another" (Ephesians 4:25).

How is the good name of another injured?

The good name of our neighbor is injured by rash judgment, detraction and calumny.

Rash judgment of one's neighbor is to believe, without sufficient reason, something harmful to another's character.

Detraction is to make known the hidden faults of another without a good reason.

Calumny, instead, is to injure the good name of another by lying.

When are we obliged to keep a secret?

We are obliged, under pain of sin, to keep a secret when our office requires it, or when the good of another demands it.

CHARITY MUST EXTEND TO ALL

"The Christian faithful should be inspired by that charity with which God has loved us, and with which He wills that we should love one another (cf. 1 John 4:11). Christian charity truly extends to all, without distinction of race, creed, or social condition: it looks for neither gain nor gratitude. For as God loved us with an unselfish love, so also the faithful should in their charity care for the human person himself, loving him with the same affection with which God sought out man. Just as Christ, then, went about all the towns and villages, curing every kind of disease and infirmity as a sign that the kingdom of God had come (cf. Matthew 9:35ff.; Acts 10:38), so also the Church, through her children, is one with men of every condition, but especially with the poor and the afflicted. For them she gladly spends and is spent (cf. 2 Corinthians 12:15), sharing in their joys and sorrows, knowing of their longings and problems, suffering with them in death's anxieties. To those in quest of peace, she wishes to answer in fraternal dialogue, bearing them the peace and the light of the Gospel."

— DECREE ON MISSION ACTIVITY OF CHURCH

KNOWING AND RESPECTING TRUTH

"The source and root of all evils which affect individuals, peoples and nations with a kind of poison and confuse the minds of many is this: ignorance of the truth—and not only ignorance, but at times a contempt for, and deliberate turning away from it.

"This is the source of all manner of errors which, like contagious diseases, pass deep into minds and into the very bloodstream of human society, and turn everything upside down with serious damage to all individuals and to the whole human race.

"Yet God endowed us with a mind capable of grasping natural truth. If we follow it, we follow God Himself, its Creator and the Guide and Lawgiver of our life. But if from lack of interest, laziness or even wickedness of mind, we turn away from it we are turning our minds from the highest Good itself and from the norm of right living....

"Those who deliberately and wantonly attack the known truth, and in their speech, writing and acting employ the weapons of falsehood in order to attract and win over uneducated people, to mold the inexperienced and impressionable minds of the young and fashion them to their own way of thought, certainly are abusing the ignorance and innocence of others and engaging in a practice wholly to be condemned."

—JOHN XXIII, ENCYCLICAL, NEAR THE CHAIR OF PETER

THE CHURCH, TEACHER
OF PRAYER

Priests must instruct their people to offer to God the Father the Divine Victim in the Sacrifice of the Mass, and to join to it the offering of their own lives. In the spirit of Christ the Shepherd, they must prompt their people to confess their sins with a contrite heart in the sacrament of Penance, so that, mindful of His words: "Repent for the kingdom of God is at hand" (Matthew 4:17), they are drawn closer to the Lord more and more each day. Priests likewise must instruct their people to participate in the celebrations of the Sacred Liturgy in such a way that they become proficient in genuine prayer. They must coax their people on to an ever more perfect and constant spirit of prayer for every grace and need.

Decree on the Ministry and Life of Priests

187

Why is the Church the teacher of prayer?

The Church is the teacher of prayer because she decides and ordains, through the mandate of Jesus Christ and therefore infallibly, what acts of worship are pleasing to God and honor the divine Majesty; she unites the faithful to the Lord and sanctifies them; finally she communicates grace, the life of the soul, particularly with the sacraments of Baptism and the Holy Eucharist.

What is grace?

Grace is a supernatural gift of God bestowed on us through the merits of Jesus Christ for our salvation, for we cannot live as good Christians and merit heaven only through our own strength.

Is there more than one kind of grace?

There are two kinds of grace: sanctifying or habitual grace and actual grace.

What is the importance of sanctifying grace?

Sanctifying grace is that grace which confers on our souls a new life, that is, a sharing in the life of God Himself, and renders us capable of

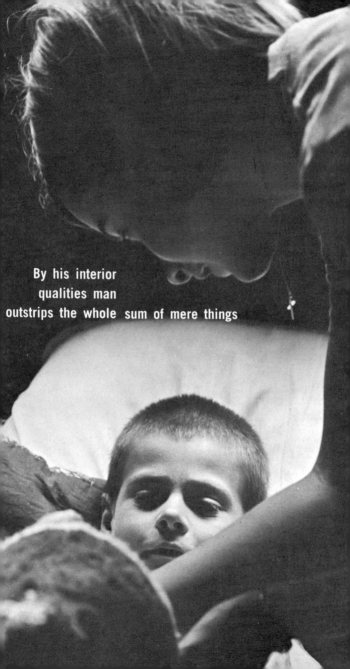

By his interior
qualities man
outstrips the whole sum of mere things

performing supernatural and meritorious acts.

Sanctifying grace makes us living temples of the Holy Spirit, adopted children of God, brothers of Jesus Christ and heirs of heaven.

Our actions merit heaven when they are performed in the state of grace and with the intention of pleasing God.

If we should have the misfortune of losing the grace of God, that is, supernatural life, with a mortal sin, we can still re-acquire it with a perfect act of contrition and through the sacrament of Penance.

What is actual grace?

Actual grace is a supernatural help from God, internal to us and of a passing nature, whereby God helps us to avoid sin, or enables us to perform actions which tend toward our salvation.

Through which channels does grace come to us?

The chief channels of grace are the seven sacraments.

Which are the seven sacraments and what is the purpose of each?

"Incorporated in the Church through **Baptism**, the faithful are destined by the baptismal character for the worship of the Christian religion; reborn as sons of God they must confess before men the faith which they have received from God through the Church.

"They are more perfectly bound to the Church by the sacrament of **Confirmation**, and the Holy Spirit endows them with special strength so that they are more strictly obliged to spread and defend the faith, both by word and by deed, as true witnesses of Christ.

"Taking part in the Eucharistic Sacrifice, which is the fount and apex of the whole Christian life, they offer the Divine Victim to God, and offer themselves along with It. Thus both by reason of the offering and through **Holy Communion** all take part in this liturgical service, not indeed, all in the same way but each in that way which is proper to himself. Strengthened in Holy Communion by the body of Christ, they then manifest in a concrete way that unity of the People of God which is suitably signified and wondrously brought about by this most august sacrament.

"Those who approach the sacrament of **Penance** obtain pardon from the mercy of God for the offence committed against Him and are at the same time reconciled with the Church, which they have wounded by their sins, and which by charity, example, and prayer seeks their conversion.

"By the sacred **Anointing of the Sick** and the prayer of her priests the whole Church commends the sick to the suffering and glorified Lord, asking that He may lighten their suffering and save them; she exhorts them, moreover, to contribute to the welfare of the whole People of God by associating themselves freely with the passion and death of Christ.

"Those of the faithful who are consecrated by **Holy Orders** are appointed to feed the Church in Christ's name with the word and the grace of God.

"Finally, Christian spouses, in virtue of the sacrament of **Matrimony,** whereby they signify and partake of the mystery of that unity and fruitful love which exists between Christ and His Church, help each other to attain to holiness in their married life and in the rearing and education of their children."

— DOGMATIC CONSTITUTION ON CHURCH

Do Baptism and Confirmation make every layman an apostle?

"Every layman must appreciate the full meaning of his membership in the Church, of his incorporation by Baptism into the living body of Christ, a royal and priestly society; of his promotion by Confirmation to the rank of responsibility of a true apostle, an official witness of divine truth, not in the strict sense of the sacramental priesthood, but in the proper sphere of the layman's life, not at the altar of the Church, but in the sanctuary of the home, not from the pulpit, but from every single vantage open to the layman in the associations of his private and public life. No less than the ordained priest, the layman has a religious vocation, a mission, a mandate to speak and work for Christ."

— BISHOP LEO J. PURSLEY

What is the Mass?

"The Mass, the Lord's Supper, is at the same time and inseparably:

"— A sacrifice in which the Sacrifice of the Cross is perpetuated;

"— A memorial of the death and resurrection of the Lord, who said 'do this in memory of me' (Luke 22:19);

"— A sacred banquet in which, through the communion of the body and blood of the Lord, the People of God share the benefits of the Paschal Sacrifice, renew the New Covenant which God has made with man once for all through the blood of Christ, and in faith and hope foreshadow and anticipate the eschatological banquet in the kingdom of the Father, proclaiming the Lord's death 'till His coming.'"

— INSTRUCTION ON WORSHIP OF EUCHARISTIC MYSTERY

"The Lord Jesus, on the night he was betrayed, took bread, and giving thanks broke, and said, 'This is my body which shall be given up for you; do this in remembrance of me.' In like manner also the cup, after he had supped, saying, 'This cup is the new covenant in my blood; do this as often as you drink it, in remembrance of me. For as often as you shall eat this bread and drink the cup, you proclaim the death of the Lord, until he comes'" (1 Corinthians 11:23-26).

What is meant by the 'real presence' of Christ in the Eucharist?

"This presence is called 'real'—by which it is not intended to exclude all other types of presence as if they could not be 'real' too, but because it is presence in the fullest sense: that is to say, it is a substantial presence by which Christ, the God-Man, is wholly and entirely present."   — PAUL VI, ENCYCLICAL, MYSTERY OF FAITH

What reverence is due to the Blessed Sacrament outside of Mass?

"In the course of the day the faithful should not omit to visit the Blessed Sacrament, which according to the liturgical laws must be kept in the churches with great reverence in a most honorable location. Such visits are a proof of gratitude, an expression of love, an acknowledgment of the Lord's presence."

—PAUL VI, ENCYCLICAL, MYSTERY OF FAITH

What is Penance or confession?

Penance or confession is the sacrament by which sins committed after Baptism are forgiven through the absolution of the priest. The priest has the power to forgive sins from Jesus Christ, who said to His apostles and to their successors in the priesthood: "Receive the Holy Spirit; whose sins you shall forgive, they are forgiven them; and whose sins you shall retain, they are retained" (John 20:22-23).

What is sin?

Sin is a voluntary disobedience of the law of God. Sin is committed when one knows that a thing is forbidden and does it just the same. There are two kinds of sin: mortal and venial.

Temptation is not a sin unless consented to.

What is mortal sin?

Mortal sin is committed when one disobeys the law of God in grievous matter, with full knowledge and deliberate consent.

This sin is called mortal, because it removes the life of grace from the soul, renders us enemies of God and merits for us the pains of hell.

If one has had the misfortune of committing a mortal sin, he must make an act of contrition, confess himself and take the necessary means to avoid sinning again.

"Take care that you are always, always in a state of grace! (cf. 1 Cor. 11:28) And do not follow those who, on the pretext of ridding the conscience of useless anxieties and troublesome scruples, try to persuade you that there is no need to be in a state of grace before receiving Holy Communion, or in order to live as honest Christians!"

— POPE PAUL VI, MAY 26, 1971

What is venial sin?

A venial sin is committed when one disobeys the law of God in a less serious matter or even in a grievous matter without full knowledge and deliberate consent of the will.

Venial sin does not destroy the life of grace, but it is an offense to God and it weakens our friendship with Him. It also disposes us to mortal sin and merits for us some temporal punishment either in this life or in the next.

What are the capital vices?

An evil inclination which leads one to commit a sin is called a vice.

There are some vices which are the source of all our sins; these are called capital vices. They are also called capital sins, even though they are not, strictly speaking, sins.

The capital vices are seven: pride, covetousness, lust, anger, gluttony, envy, sloth.

Which sins are we obliged to confess?

We are obliged to confess all our mortal sins, telling their kind, the number of times we have committed each sin, and any circumstances changing their nature.

It is not necessary to confess our venial sins, but it is well to do so.

Why is it well to confess venial sins?

"Venial sins may be expiated in many ways which are to be highly commended. But to ensure more rapid progress day by day in the path of virtue, We will that the pious practice of frequent confession, which was introduced into the Church by the inspiration of the Holy Spirit, should be earnestly advocated. By it genuine self-knowledge is increased, Christian humility grows, bad habits are corrected, spiritual neglect and tepidity are resisted, the conscience is purified, the will strengthened, a salutary self-control is attained, and grace is increased in virtue of the sacrament itself."

— PIUS XII, ENCYCLICAL, MYSTICAL BODY OF CHRIST

What are indulgences?

An indulgence is the remission granted by the Church of the temporal punishment due to sins already forgiven.

A plenary indulgence is the remission of all the temporal punishment due to our sins, if the dispositions of the soul are perfect.

A partial indulgence, instead, is the remission of part of the temporal punishment due to our sins.

To gain an indulgence for ourselves we must be in the state of grace, have at least a general intention of gaining the indulgence, and perform the works required by the Church.

Does the spiritual life consist entirely in participating at Mass and receiving the sacraments?

"The spiritual life is not limited solely to participation in the liturgy. The Christian is indeed called to pray with his brethren, but he must also enter into his chamber to pray to the Father, in secret; yet more, according to the teaching of the Apostle, he should pray without ceasing.

"We learn from the same Apostle that we must always bear about in our body the dying of Jesus, so that the life also of Jesus may be made manifest in our bodily frame. This is why we ask the Lord in the sacrifice of the Mass that, 'receiving the offering of the spiritual victim,' He may fashion us for Himself 'as an eternal gift.'"

— CONSTITUTION ON SACRED LITURGY

With what dispositions should we pray?

Attention, that is, reflection on what we are saying in order to understand the prayer that we are reciting and to be attentive to divine inspirations.

Humility. St. Augustine says that, with respect to God, we are beggars, and must implore through His mercy that which we cannot obtain through justice.

Confidence, that confidence which does not base itself on our merits, but on the infinite goodness of God and on the merits of Jesus Christ. Each one of us is answered in proportion to the confidence he has in God.

Perseverance. At times it seems that God is not listening to our prayers, because He wants our prayer to be persevering.

Does God always answer our prayers?

God always answers our prayers when we have prayed properly, and when what we ask for is something really good for us.

First of all we must ask God for spiritual graces, because these are the most important, since our soul is superior to our body. In the second place, we may also ask for temporal graces insofar as they will be truly useful to us.

God answers all our prayers in the way that is best for us; thus, when we do not receive what we ask for, we receive something better for our welfare.

What are sacramentals?

Sacramentals are holy things or actions of which the Church makes use to obtain for us from God, through her intercession, spiritual and temporal favors. Among these are liturgical rites, various blessings and devotions.

THE EUCHARIST

"We believe that the Mass, celebrated by the priest representing the person of Christ by virtue of the power received through the sacrament of Orders, and offered by him in the name of Christ and the members of His Mystical Body, is the sacrifice of Calvary rendered sacramentally present on our altars.

"We believe that as the bread and wine consecrated by the Lord at the Last Supper were changed into His body and His blood which were to be offered for us on the cross, likewise the bread and wine consecrated by the priest are changed into the body and blood of Christ enthroned gloriously in heaven, and we believe that the mysterious presence of the Lord, under what continues to appear to our senses as before, is a true, real and substantial presence.

"Christ cannot be thus present in this sacrament except by the change into His body of the reality itself of the bread and the change into His blood of the reality itself of the wine, leaving unchanged only the properties of the bread and wine which our senses perceive. This mysterious change is very appropriately called by the Church **transubstantiation.** Every theological explanation which seeks some understanding of this mystery must, in order to be in accord with Catholic faith, maintain that in the reality itself, independently of our mind, the bread and wine have ceased to exist after the Consecration, so that it is the adorable body and blood of the Lord Jesus that from then on are really before us under the sacramental species of bread and wine, as the Lord willed it, in order to give Himself to us as food and to associate us with the unity of His Mystical Body.

"The unique and indivisible existence of the Lord glorious in heaven is not multiplied, but is rendered present by the sacrament in the many places on earth where Mass is celebrated. And this existence remains present, after the sacrifice, in the Blessed Sacrament which is, in the tabernacle, the living heart of each of our churches. And it is our very sweet duty to honor and adore in the blessed Host which our eyes see, the Incarnate Word whom they cannot see, and who, without leaving heaven, is made present before us."

—PAUL VI, CREDO OF PEOPLE OF GOD

PRAYER—PUBLIC AND PRIVATE

"The divine Redeemer is most closely united not only with His Church, which is His beloved Spouse, but also with each and every one of the faithful, and He ardently desires to speak with them heart to heart, especially after Holy Communion. It is true that public prayer, inasmuch as it is offered by Mother Church, excels any other kind of prayer by reason of her dignity as Spouse of Christ; but no prayer, even the most private, is lacking in dignity or power, and all prayer is of the greatest help to the Mystical Body in which, through the Communion of Saints, no good can be done, no virtue practised by individual members, which does not redound also to the salvation of all.

Neither is a man forbidden to ask for himself particular favors even for this life merely because he is a member of this Body, provided he is always resigned to the divine will; for the members retain their own personality and remain subject to their own individual needs. Moreover, how highly all should esteem mental prayer is proved not only by ecclesiastical documents but also by the custom and practice of the saints.''

— PIUS XII, ENCYCLICAL, MYSTICAL BODY OF CHRIST

THE APOSTOLIC COLLEGE

Jesus Christ, the eternal Shepherd, established His holy Church, having sent forth the apostles as He Himself had been sent by the Father; and He willed that their successors, namely the bishops, should be shepherds in His Church even to the consummation of the world. And in order that the episcopate itself might be one and undivided, He placed blessed Peter over the other apostles, and instituted in him a permanent and visible source and foundation of unity of faith and communion.

—Dogmatic Constitution on Church

You are Peter and upon this rock I will build my Church, and the gates of hell shall not prevail against it. And I will give you the keys of the kingdom of heaven; and whatever you shall bind on earth shall be bound in heaven, and whatever you shall loose on earth shall be loosed in heaven.

—Matthew 16:18-19

Who has supreme power in the entire Church?
"In this Church of Christ the Roman Pontiff, as the successor of Peter, to whom Christ entrusted the feeding of His sheep and lambs, enjoys supreme, full, immediate power in the universal authority over the care of souls by divine institution. Therefore, as pastor of all the faithful, he is sent to provide for the common good of the universal Church and for the good of the individual churches. Hence, he holds a primacy of ordinary power over all the churches."

— DECREE CONCERNING PASTORAL OFFICE OF BISHOPS IN CHURCH

What is the Roman Curia?
"In exercising supreme, full, and immediate power in the universal Church, the Roman Pontiff makes use of the departments of the Roman Curia which, therefore, perform their duties in his name and with his authority for the good of the churches and in the service of the sacred pastors."

— DECREE CONCERNING PASTORAL OFFICE OF BISHOPS IN CHURCH

Which are the maximum powers of the Pope?
The maximum powers of the Pope are the supreme infallible magisterium or teaching

authority; the supreme power of government; the supreme power in the order of sanctification. The totality of these powers is called primacy over each and every bishop; over all the rites; over all the churches and over all the faithful considered both individually as well as collectively.

In the Church, to whom does the power of teaching belong?

The power of teaching in the Church belongs to the Pope and to the body of the bishops united with him. Such power is exercised in an infallible manner. Although no bishop possesses personal infallibility, when all are united with the Pope, their head, they are infallible.

In what form is such power exercised?

The power of teaching is exercised by the Church in an **ordinary** form, by means of preaching and in a **solemn** form, by means of pontifical definitions and ecumenical councils. The ecumenical or general council is the assembly of the episcopal body under the authority of the Pope, and the definition and dispositions will have value only if confirmed by him.

What does supreme infallible magisterium mean?

Supreme infallible magisterium means that when the Pope, as head of the Church, speaks **ex cathedra**, he enjoys alone the very infallibility conceded to all the Church united.

(**Infallibility** is not to be confused with **impeccability**, that is, with absolute sinlessness.)

When does the Pope speak ex cathedra?

The Pope speaks **ex cathedra** only when these four conditions are verified all together: 1) he acts as supreme shepherd in virtue of his office and apostolic authority; 2) he defines doctrines of faith or morals; 3) he intends to give a dogmatic definition which is to be held as a truth of faith; and 4) the definition is to bind all the members of the Church.

Might not a papal directive be unacceptable in conscience?

"It is unacceptable to affirm that the Pope indicates a norm of moral conduct that is in conflict with the carrying out of other moral duties. The law of God is consistent in everything: it is the Truth."

— ARCHBISHOP COVARRUBIAS, VALPARAISO, CHILE

Upon what is pontifical infallibility based?

Pontifical infallibility is not based on the particular capabilities or learning of the Pontiff, but rather on the particular assistance of the Holy Spirit and upon the special office of supreme shepherd of the flock of Jesus Christ, which Peter, in the name of the Divine Master, must lead to the salutary pastures of truth and of holiness.

Which are the special promises made by Jesus Christ to Peter?

There are three promises in particular of this

special assistance made to Peter and to his successors: 1) Peter was established as the foundation of the Church: "You are Peter, and upon this rock I will build my Church" (Matthew 16:18); 2) Jesus Christ said special prayers for him: "I have prayed for you, Peter, that your faith may not fail; and do you ... strengthen your brethren" (Luke 22:32); 3) Peter received the supreme power to feed all the flock of Christ: "Feed my lambs, ... feed my sheep" (John 21:15-17). The office of feeding the entire flock is incompatible with the possibility of teaching error. Moreover, to Peter were consigned the keys of the kingdom of heaven: what he decides is ratified in heaven. How could God ratify error? "I will give you the keys of the kingdom of heaven; and whatever you shall bind on earth shall be bound in heaven, and whatever you shall loose on earth shall be loosed in heaven" (Matthew 16:19). From these four evangelical texts it is evident that Christ and Peter form one mystical entity. To say that Peter is infallible is to say that Christ is infallible.

What does supreme power of government mean?
Supreme power of government means that while Jesus Christ conferred the power to govern on the apostles, He gave directly and immediately to only one of them, that is to Peter, the first place and the primacy over all the Church as her visible head; not merely a prerogative of honor, but as a true and proper jurisdiction.

What does such power embrace?

Such power embraces the fullness of legislative, judicial and penal authority; thus, the Pope not only gives directives and exercises a right of inspection, but he himself has the power to make laws which oblige in conscience. From the legislative power derives the power to judge upon the observance and to punish the transgressors. The maximum punishments are excommunication and interdiction.

What does supreme power in the order of sanctification mean?

Supreme power in the order of sanctification means that the Pope has the supreme power of order and of jurisdiction, and therefore, either through power of order, or through that of jurisdiction, the means of grace come and are in general regulated by him, either directly, as with the concession of the jubilee indulgence, or indirectly, as for example, the administration of the sacraments.

What follows from these principles?

From these principles it follows that everyone, pastors and faithful of every rite and of every degree, both collectively and individually, are bound to the Roman Pontiff by a true hierarchical subordination and by a true obedience, not only in that which regards faith and morals, but also in that which has to do with discipline and with the government of the Church spread throughout the world.

In what manner have the three supreme powers passed from Peter to his successors?

The three supreme powers have passed from Peter to the individual Popes by way of succession. This is clearly apparent from three truths; **first:** dogmatic truth—if the Church must last until the end of the world it is evident that the primacy of Peter must be perpetuated through the centuries and transmitted to the successors of Peter; **second:** historical truth — Peter came to Rome, was the first bishop of that city and died there; his successors are the heirs of his primacy in the Church; **third:** historical-chronological truth — the successor of Peter is the Pope at present in office.

Who are the bishops?

"Among those various ministries which, according to tradition, were exercised in the Church from the earliest times, the chief place belongs to the office of those who, appointed to the episcopate, by a succession running from the beginning, are passers-on of the apostolic seed. Thus, as St. Irenaeus testifies, through those who were appointed bishops by the apostles, and through their successors down to our time, the apostolic tradition is manifested and preserved.

"Bishops, therefore, with their helpers, the priests and deacons, have taken up the service of the community, presiding in place of God over the flock, whose shepherds they are, as teachers for doctrine, priests for sacred worship, and ministers for governing."

— DOGMATIC CONSTITUTION ON CHURCH

Is the office of bishops permanent and essential?

"Just as the office granted to Peter, the first among the apostles, is permanent and is to be transmitted to his successors, so also the apostles' office of nurturing the Church is permanent, and is to be exercised without interruption by the sacred order of bishops. Therefore, the Sacred Council teaches that bishops by divine institution have succeeded to the place of the apostles, as shepherds of the Church, and he who hears them, hears Christ, and he who rejects them, rejects Christ and Him who sent Christ."

— DOGMATIC CONSTITUTION ON CHURCH

What is meant by collegiality?

"Just as in the Gospel, the Lord so disposing, St. Peter and the other apostles constitute one apostolic college, so in a similar way the Roman Pontiff, the successor of Peter, and the bishops, the successors of the apostles, are joined together.

"Indeed, the very ancient practice whereby bishops duly established in all parts of the world were in communion with one another and with the Bishop of Rome in a bond of unity, charity and peace, and also the councils assembled together, in which more profound issues were settled in common, the opinion of the many having been prudently considered, both of these factors are already an indication of the collegiate character and aspect of the episcopal order; and the ecumenical councils held in the course of centuries are also manifest proof of that same character. . . .

"But the college or body of bishops has no authority unless it is understood together with the Roman Pontiff, the successor of Peter, as its head. The Pope's power of primacy over all, both pastors and faithful, remains whole and intact. In virtue of his office, that is as Vicar of Christ and pastor of the whole Church, the Roman Pontiff has full, supreme and universal power over the Church. And he is always free to exercise this power.

"The order of bishops, which succeeds to the college of apostles and gives this apostolic body continued existence, is also the subject of supreme and full power over the universal Church, provided we understand this body together with its head the Roman Pontiff and never without this head. This power can be exercised only with the consent of the Roman Pontiff. For our Lord placed Simon alone as the rock and the bearer of the keys of the Church, and made him shepherd of the whole flock.

"It is evident, however, that the power of binding and loosing, which was given to Peter, was granted also to the college of apostles, joined with their head. This college, insofar as it is composed of many, expresses the variety and universality of the People of God, but insofar as it is assembled under one head, it expresses the unity of the flock of Christ."

— DOGMATIC CONSTITUTION ON CHURCH

What do the individual bishops represent?

"The individual bishops represent each his own church, but all of them together and with the Pope represent the entire Church in the bond of peace, love and unity."

— DOGMATIC CONSTITUTION ON CHURCH

What is the Synod of Bishops?

"The Synod of Bishops, whereby bishops chosen from various parts of the world lend their valuable assistance to the supreme pastor of the Church, is so constituted as to be: a) a central ecclesiastical institution, b) representing the complete Catholic episcopate, c) by its nature perpetual, d) as for its structure, performing its duties for a time and when called upon. By its very nature it is the task of the Synod of Bishops to inform and give advice. It may also have a deliberative power, when such power is conferred on it by the sovereign Pontiff, who will in such cases confirm the decisions of the Synod."

POPE PAUL VI, SEPTEMBER 15, 1965

THE PRIMACY OF PETER

"After he arose from the dead, Jesus Christ manifested himself for the third time to his disciples at the sea of Tiberias.

"When, therefore, they had breakfasted, Jesus said to Simon Peter: 'Simon, son of John, do you love me more than these do?' He said to him: 'Yes, Lord, you know that I love you.' Jesus said to him: 'Feed my lambs.' He said to him a second time: 'Simon, son of John, do you love me?' Peter said to him: 'Yes, Lord, you know that I love you.' Jesus said to him: 'Feed my lambs.' A third time he said to him: 'Simon, son of John, do you love me?' Peter was grieved because he said to him, for the third time: 'Do you love me?' And he said to him: 'Lord, you know all things, you know that I love you.' Jesus said to him: 'Feed my sheep'' (John 21:15-17).

"O Lord, graciously look down upon the Pastor and ruler of all the faithful, Your servant, to whom You willed to entrust Your Church; grant to him, we beseech You, to be of help with example and with word to those of whom he is the head, so that he may arrive at eternal life together with the flock entrusted to him. Amen."

— THE LITURGY

THE CHARISM OF INFALLIBILITY

"Although the individual bishops do not enjoy the prerogative of infallibility, they nevertheless proclaim Christ's doctrine infallibly whenever, even though dispersed through the world, but still maintaining the bond of communion among themselves and with the successor of Peter, and authentically teaching matters of faith and morals, they are in agreement on one position as definitively to be held. This is even more clearly verified when, gathered together in an ecumenical council, they are teachers and judges of faith and morals for the universal Church, whose definitions must be adhered to with the submission of faith.

"The infallibility with which the Divine Redeemer willed His Church to be endowed in defining doctrine of faith and morals, extends as far as the deposit of Revelation extends, which must be religiously guarded and faithfully expounded.

"And this is the infallibility which the Roman Pontiff, the head of the college of bishops, enjoys in virtue of his office, when, as the supreme shepherd and teacher of all the faithful, who confirms his brethren in their faith, by a definitive act he proclaims a doctrine of faith or morals. And therefore his definitions, of themselves, and not from the consent of the Church, are justly styled irreformable, since they are pronounced with the assistance of the Holy Spirit, promised to him in blessed Peter, and therefore they need no approval of others, nor do they allow an appeal to any other judgment. For then the Roman Pontiff is not pronouncing judgment as a private person, but as the supreme teacher of the universal Church, in whom the charism of infallibility of the Church itself is individually present, he is expounding or defending a doctrine of Catholic faith.

"The infallibility promised to the Church resides also in the body of bishops, when that body exercises the supreme magisterium with the successor of Peter. To these definitions the assent of the Church can never be wanting, on account of the activity of that same Holy Spirit, by which the whole flock of Christ is preserved and progresses in unity of faith."

— DOGMATIC CONSTITUTION ON CHURCH

THE STRUCTURE OF THE CHURCH

"The Scriptures tell us that Jesus went about preaching the Kingdom of God. That Kingdom, present in His Church, does not hover form-lessly over the cities or exist unseen among the nations of the world. The People of God, the Body of Christ, the Temple of the Spirit, His Church is organized, structured, visible. The visibility of the Church is essential to her identity and is, indeed, a sign, in this case sacramental, of something divine. The Church is a visible sign of the mystery of God, the mystery of grace, the mystery of Christ and of the Spirit.

"When one realizes that the visibility of the Church is achieved through human persons and human signs, then one understands why her visibility will be inadequate to the task of signifying all that must be signified. None-theless, the visibility of the Church is a sign, a sacrament, an instrument through which God acts and dwells with us.

"If one reflects on how detached from human history and how inconsistent with the human condition an invisible Church would be, he realizes how necessary is that visibility which Catholics have always believed to be Christ's own provision for His Church.

"This does not mean that visibility is merely the best of many possible choices. Nor does it mean that visibility is something for which we settle either for reasons of convenience or because there is nothing else available. It does not mean, finally, that visibility is something extrinsic to the Church, a ceremonial addition or a pragmatic necessity, something the Church might have done without or may yet do without, or even something which is not really the Church, as if the real Church were to be found only on an invisible level eluding and resisting all the visible structures of community.

"If this latter concept were well-founded, then there would, in effect, be two Churches. One would be invisible and therein alone the reality of the Church would be accessible to us or at least to some of us; the other, visible, would somehow parallel the invisible Church, being tolerable when useful for the less enlightened, but not for those who, as in every form of Gnosticism, think of themselves as a religious elite and deprecate the need for a visible or, as they sometimes say, institutional Church.

"The visibility which is Christ's intention for His Church is explained by none of the above. The visible structuring of the Church is no less the Church than her invisible reality. The sacramental Church is the spontaneous result of grace which, like love, seeks visible expression and identifies with it. The grace of Christ in which the Church is created is not

If I had not known the Christ,
God would have been for me
a meaningless word;
the Infinite Being
would have been unimaginable.

imprisoned in the visible structure of the Church, but neither is it independent of her. For the Church is a sign or sacrament of grace.

"This means that the grace of the Lord, requiring visible presence among us (even as did He), is destined to triumph when time shall be no more and is expressed through the institutional structures of the Church and is inseparable from them. This is not to say that grace, salvation, or the Kingdom of God is found only **where** the organized Church is seen to be at work, but it is to say that all grace seeks to become manifest not only in the Incarnation of Christ, but also in those visible elements of His Church which are not merely human but sacramental in the fullest sense of the word.

"As is a sacrament, the Church is the result of grace, an intensification of grace and an effective sign of grace at work among us. One who belongs to the Church through faith, hope and charity has found where God's graces converge concretely. In the visible Church, grace is given an earthly habitation and a name; in the visible Church, Christ's victorious saving presence is recognized and celebrated; in the visible Church, the invisible mystery of the Church achieves its history."

—U.S. BISHOPS' PASTORAL LETTER, CHURCH IN OUR DAY

SHE GAVE LIFE
TO THE WORLD

Hail, full of grace, the Lord is with you. Blessed are you among women and blessed is the fruit of your womb.
— Luke 1:28, 42

The Virgin Mary, who at the message of the angel, received the Word of God in her heart and in her body and gave Life to the world, is acknowledged and honored as being truly the Mother of God and Mother of the Redeemed.
— Dogmatic Constitution on Church

In what manner did the Son of God come on earth?
The Son of God came on earth by taking on human flesh in the all-pure womb of the Virgin Mary by the power of the Holy Spirit. Just as a woman, Eve, was the beginning of our ruin through Adam, so a woman, Mary, was the beginning of our salvation through her divine Son, Jesus Christ.

What is meant by saying that Mary is our Mediatrix?
As Mary was the Mother of Christ, so she was made the mother of all the followers of Jesus. As we have a Mediator before the Father, who is Jesus Christ, so we have a Mediatrix before the Son: Mary Most Holy.

What is the true reason for the greatness, the privileges and the role of Mary?
The true reason for the greatness, the privileges, and the role of Mary is the fact that she is the true **Mother of God.** This title of the divine motherhood of Mary is the foundation and the cause of all her other privileges.

Which are the privileges of Mary?
Mary's privileges can be listed as follows: she is called and is the true Mother of God; consequently she is our spiritual mother; she was conceived immaculate—exempt, that is, from original sin; she was a virgin before, during and after the birth of Christ; she attained to a very special holiness; she was assumed into heaven body and soul; she is the universal Mediatrix and dispenser of grace.

What is Mary's relationship with us?
Mary is the true spiritual mother of mankind as she was the true mother of Jesus; she was the cooperator with Christ in the work of the redemption, therefore she is our co-redemptrix; she is Queen of mankind and of every creature.

What should be our devotion to Mary?
To Mary must be given the cult of hyperdulia, that is, superior to that given the angels and the saints, but inferior to that given God. This devotion embraces knowledge, veneration, prayer, love and imitation.

What are the good effects of devotion to Mary?
The good effects of devotion to Mary are innumerable, both spiritual and material, private and public—particularly those indicated by St. Pius X: the formation of Jesus in each soul and the Christianization of the world.

What is Mary's special relationship to Christian apostles?
Mary gave the world the Divine Master, Jesus

Christ, who gave her to the apostles of all times as Mother, Teacher and Queen.

What is the Rosary?

"The Rosary...is a very excellent means of prayer and meditation in the form of a mystical crown in which the prayers 'Our Father,' 'Hail Mary' and 'Glory be to the Father' are intertwined with meditation on the greatest mysteries of our faith and which presents to the mind, like many pictures, the drama of the Incarnation of our Lord and the Redemption."

— JOHN XXIII, ENCYCLICAL, GRATEFUL MEMORY

"The Rosary offers an easy way to penetrate the chief mysteries of the Christian religion and to impress them upon the mind.

"To ward off the exceedingly great dangers of ignorance from her children, the Church, which never relaxes her vigilant and diligent care, has been in the habit of looking for the staunchest support of faith in the Rosary of Mary."

— LEO XIII, ENCYCLICAL, MAGNAE DEI MATRIS

In the recitation of the Rosary, why are certain prayers repeated?

"Vocal prayer harmonizes with the mysteries. First, as is fitting and right, comes the Lord's Prayer, addressed to Our Father in heaven. Having, with the petitions dictated by our Divine Master, called upon the Father, from the throne of His Majesty, we turn our prayerful voices to Mary. Thus is confirmed that law of merciful mediation of which we have spoken, and which St. Bernardine of Siena thus expresses: 'Every grace granted to man has three successive steps: By God it is communicated to Christ, from Christ it passes to the Virgin, and from the Virgin it descends to us.' And we, by the very form of the Rosary, do linger longest and as it were, by preference upon the last and lowest of these steps; repeating by decades the Angelic Salutation, so that with greater confidence we may thence attain to the higher degrees—that is, may rise, by means of Christ, to the divine Father.

"For if we thus again and again greet Mary, it is precisely that our failing and defective prayers may be strengthened with the necessary confidence; confidence which rises in us in thinking that Mary more than praying for us prays to God in our name."

—LEO XIII, ENCYCLICAL, JUCUNDA SEMPER

What other influence does Mary exercise on redeemed mankind?

"The cooperation of the Mother of the Church in the development of the divine life of souls does not come to an end with the appeal to the Son. She exercises on redeemed men another influence: that of example. An influence which is indeed most important, according to the well-known axiom: 'Words move, examples attract.' In fact, just as the teachings of the parents become far more efficacious if they are strengthened by the example of a life conforming with the norms of human and Christian prudence, so the sweetness and the enchantment emanating from the sublime virtues of the immaculate Mother of God attract souls in an irresistible way to imitation of the divine model, Jesus Christ, of whom she was the most faithful image."

—PAUL VI, ENCYCLICAL, THE GREAT SIGN

THE ANNUNCIATION

"The angel Gabriel was sent from God to a town of Galilee called Nazareth, to a virgin betrothed to a man named Joseph, of the house of David, and the virgin's name was Mary. And when the angel had come to her, he said: Hail, full of grace, the Lord is with you. Blessed are you among women. When she had heard him she was troubled at his word, and kept pondering what manner of greeting this might be.

"And the angel said to her: Do not be afraid, Mary, for you have found grace with God. Behold, you shall conceive in your womb and shall bring forth a son; and you shall call his name Jesus...; and of his kingdom there shall be no end. But Mary said to the angel: How shall this happen, since I know not man? And the angel answered and said to her: The Holy Spirit shall come upon you and the power of the Most High shall overshadow you, and therefore the Holy One to be born shall be called the Son of God.... But Mary said: Behold the handmaid of the Lord; be it done to me according to your word" (Luke 1:26-38).

MARY IN THE LIFE OF THE CHURCH

"There is but one Mediator as we know from the words of the Apostle, 'for there is one God and one Mediator of God and men, the man Christ Jesus, who gave himself a redemption for all.' The maternal duty of Mary toward men in no wise obscures or diminishes this unique mediation of Christ, but rather shows His power. For all the salvific influence of the Blessed Virgin on men originates, not from some inner necessity, but from the divine pleasure. It flows forth from the superabundance of the merits of Christ, rests on His mediation, depends entirely on it and draws all its power from it. In no way does it impede, but rather does it foster the immediate union of the faithful with Christ.

"Predestined from eternity by that decree of divine Providence which determined the Incarnation of the Word to be the Mother of God, the Blessed Virgin was on this earth the virgin Mother of the Redeemer, and above all others and in a singular way the generous associate and humble handmaid of the Lord. She conceived, brought forth, and nourished Christ, she presented Him to the Father in the temple, and was united with Him by compassion as He died on the cross. In this singular way she cooperated by her obedience, faith, hope and burning charity in the work of the Savior in giving back supernatural life to souls. Wherefore she is our mother in the order of grace.

"This maternity of Mary in the order of grace began with the consent which she gave in faith at the Annunciation and which she sustained without wavering beneath the cross, and lasts until the eternal fulfillment of all the elect. Taken up to heaven she did not lay aside this salvific duty, but by her constant intercession continued to bring us the gifts of eternal salvation. By her maternal charity, she cares for the brethren of her Son, who still journey on earth surrounded by dangers and difficulties, until they are led into the happiness of their true home."

—DOGMATIC CONSTITUTION ON CHURCH

STAR OF THE SEA

"O whoever you are who, in the sea of this world, feel yourself rather tossed about between storms and tempests than walking on the earth, do not look away from the brightness of this Star if you do not want to be submerged by the waves.

"If the winds of temptation blow, if you stumble against the reefs of tribulations, look at the Star, call Mary. If you are agitated by waves of pride, of ambition, of murmuring, of envy, look at the Star, call Mary. If anger or avarice or seduction of the flesh agitate the fragile ship of the soul, look at the Star, call Mary. If disturbed by the enormity of crimes, confused by the guilt of soul, terrified by the severity of the judgment, you feel yourself pulled into the vortex of melancholy, into the abyss of despair, think of Mary.

"In dangers, in troubles, in doubts think of Mary, call Mary. Let her not depart from your lips, let her not depart from your heart; and to obtain the help of her prayers, do not lose sight of the examples of her life. Following her you do not go astray; by praying to her you do not despair; thinking of her you do not err. If she upholds you, you do not fall; if she protects you, you have nothing to fear; if she accompanies you, you do not tire; if she is propitious to you, you will arrive at the goal and thus experience, in yourself, how rightly it was said: 'and the virgin's name was Mary.'"

—ST. BERNARD

Basic Catholic Prayers

THE SIGN OF THE CROSS

In the name of the Father, and of the Son, and of the Holy Spirit. Amen.

THE LORD'S PRAYER

Our Father, who art in heaven, hallowed be Thy name; Thy kingdom come; Thy will be done on earth as it is in heaven. Give us this day our daily bread; and forgive us our trespasses as we forgive those who trespass against us; and lead us not into temptation, but deliver us from evil. Amen.

THE HAIL MARY

Hail Mary, full of grace! the Lord is with thee; blessed art thou among women, and blessed is the fruit of thy womb, Jesus. Holy Mary, Mother of God, pray for us sinners, now and at the hour of our death. Amen.

GLORY BE TO THE FATHER

Glory be to the Father, and to the Son, and to the Holy Spirit. As it was in the beginning, is now, and ever shall be, world without end. Amen.

THE APOSTLES' CREED

I believe in God, the Father Almighty, Creator of heaven and earth; and in Jesus Christ, His only Son, Our Lord; who was conceived by the Holy Spirit, born of the Virgin Mary, suffered under Pontius Pilate, was crucified, died, and was buried. He descended into hell; the third day he arose again from the dead; He ascended into heaven, sits at the right hand of God, the Father Almighty; from thence He shall come to judge the living and the dead. I believe in the Holy Spirit, the Holy Catholic Church, the communion of saints, the forgiveness of sins, the resurrection of the body, and life everlasting. Amen.

AN ACT OF FAITH

O my God, I firmly believe that You are one God in three Divine Persons, Father, Son, and Holy Spirit; I believe that Your Divine Son became man and died for our sins, and that He will come to judge the living and the dead. I believe these and all the truths which the Holy Catholic Church teaches, because You have revealed them, who can neither deceive nor be deceived.

AN ACT OF HOPE

O my God, relying on Your infinite goodness and promises, I hope to obtain pardon of my sins, the help of Your grace, and life everlasting, through the merits of Jesus Christ, my Lord and Redeemer.

AN ACT OF LOVE

O my God, I love You above all things, with my whole heart and soul, because You are all-good and worthy of all love. I love my neighbor as myself for the love of You. I forgive all who have injured me, and I ask pardon of all whom I have injured.

AN ACT OF CONTRITION

O my God, I am heartily sorry for having offended You, and I detest all my sins, because of Your just punishments, but most of all because they offend You, my God, who are all-good and deserving of all my love. I firmly resolve, with the help of Your grace, to sin no more and to avoid the near occasions of sin.

QUESTIONS FOR REVIEW AND DISCUSSION

ORIGIN OF THINGS

1. How do we know that the universe had a beginning through creation?
2. What do reason and science tell us about creation?

WHAT IS MAN?

1. How do we know that the human soul exists?
2. What does Revelation tell us about man's origin and make up?
3. What does the Church hold regarding the origin of the human soul?
4. What do the soul's own activities tell us about it?

MAN'S LOFTY DESTINY

1. How do we know that man's soul is immortal and that human life has a purpose?
2. Why can complete happiness be attained only in the next life?
3. How should man view the present life and earthly progress?
4. What is the relationship between a person's actions and his future beyond the grave?

A PERSONAL, PROVIDENT GOD

1. How do we know that there is a God?
2. Can an atheist be a true humanist?
3. How do we know that God is one, changeless and perfect?
4. What do we know about the providence of God?
5. What is faith? How important is it?

RESPONSE TO THE CREATOR'S LOVE

1. In what does religion consist?
2. Why is religion important to man?
3. How is supernatural religion superior to natural religion?
4. What is worship?

EVER IN GOD'S CARE

1. What special gifts did our first parents receive from God?
2. What is meant by original sin?
3. How did God help man after his fall?

MEN OF GOD

1. What do we mean by inspired writings?
2. Why are miracles and prophecies important with regard to Sacred Scripture?
3. What is the role of the Old Testament in God's plan of salvation?

WHO IS JESUS CHRIST?

1. How do the Scriptures and the history of Christianity prove the divinity of Jesus Christ?
2. How are Christ's teachings related to those of the Old Testament?

3. How do we show that the Gospels are true, historical documents?
4. What is the importance of Sacred Tradition?

FOLLOWERS OF JESUS CHRIST

1. What gifts has our Savior given to us?
2. In what does Christianity consist?
3. May a Christian accept any of the teachings of secular humanism?
4. What can an ordinary Christian do to help the apostolate of the media of communication?

CHRIST'S CHURCH—HUMAN AND DIVINE

1. Why do we say that the Church is both human and divine?
2. How does the Church's interest in the temporal world differ from that of the atheist or secular humanist?
3. What relationship should religion have to everyday life?

HOW IS CHRIST'S CHURCH DISTINGUISHED?

1. What is meant by oneness, holiness, catholicity and apostolicity?
2. Is salvation outside the Church possible?
3. Has the Church anything in common with the great non-Christian religions?
4. What bonds of unity link Catholics with their separated brethren (non-Catholic Christians)?

THE CHURCH, TEACHER OF TRUTH

1. Explain why the "immutability of dogma" and the "development of doctrine" are not contradictory terms.
2. How can a Catholic be sure he is acting with an upright conscience?

THE CHURCH, TEACHER OF HOLINESS

1. Can a Christian passively conform to his environment?
2. What are our duties towards God?
3. What are our duties towards our fellow men?

THE CHURCH, TEACHER OF PRAYER

1. Why are sanctifying and actual grace important?
2. Why should the Mass and the sacraments play a key role in the life of the Christian?
3. What is the value of prayer in the Christian life?

THE APOSTOLIC COLLEGE

1. What is meant by papal primacy?
2. What is the role of the bishops in relation to the Pope?

SHE GAVE LIFE TO THE WORLD

1. Why do Catholics honor Mary?
2. What is the purpose of the Rosary?

APPENDIX

POPE CALLS FOR MISSIONARY WORKERS

February, 1971

We, Paul VI...
—Responding to the anguished voices of those eager for light who beg us: "Come across and help us" (cf. Acts 16:9)—
—We repeat the call which, from distant times, God has addressed to generous hearts: "Leave your country, your family and your father's house for the land I will show you" (Genesis 12:1)....
—**To you, young men and women,** whose heart, eager for truth, justice and love, seeks noble causes to defend by disinterested effort, we say: Listen to the call to become heralds of the Good News of Salvation; come with the riches of your faith and your youthful enthusiasm; teach men that there is a God who loves them, who waits for them, and who wishes them to be close to Him like children gathered round the head of the family; come to nurse the body, enlighten the intellect; teach how to live better and grow in humanity; and build the Church for the greater glory of God.

LAY MISSIONARY ORGANIZATIONS IN THE UNITED STATES

LAY MISSION HELPERS ASSOCIATION (Archdiocese of Los Angeles)
1531 West 9th St., Los Angeles, Calif. 90015

Length of commitment: one or more three-year terms.

Areas served: mission areas in the U.S., Canada, Africa, Latin America and the Pacific.

Type of work done: Lay Mission Helpers are nurses and all para-medical personnel; teachers; experts in cooperatives and credit unions; business administrators; accountants; secretaries; radio programmers; technicians; journalists; mechanics; carpenters; plumbers; airplane pilots and mechanics; printers; agricultural and animal husbandry experts, etc.

MISSION DOCTORS ASSOCIATION
(Same address as above)

Length of commitment: three years.

Areas served: Malawi, Rhodesia and West Indies.

Type of work done: Mission Doctors staff mission hospitals and dispensaries. They also organize and supervise the training of nurses and paramedical personnel at the place of their assignment.

INTERNATIONAL LIASON (Placement office for volunteer lay personnel—Archdiocese of Newark, N.J.)

39 Lackawanna Place, Bloomfield, N.J. 07003

Length of commitment: for service in the U.S., usually one year; for service abroad, usually two years; short term (e.g. summer vacation) volunteers also accepted.

Areas served: all states of the U.S., New Guinea, Guadalcanal; Tanzania, Zambia, Uganda, Malawi, Liberia, British Honduras, Brazil, Peru and Argentina.

Type of work done: Volunteers are nurses, teachers, doctors, carpenters, catechists, laborers, parish workers, technicians, mechanics, agronomists—people from all walks of life.

CATHOLIC MEDICAL MISSION BOARD
10 West 17th St., New York, N.Y. 10011

Length of commitment: either long or short term.
Areas served: U.S., West Indies, Africa, Latin America and Asia (21 nations in all).
Type of work done: CMMB volunteers are doctors, dentists, nurses, technicians and all types of para-medical personnel.

SOCIETY OF OUR LADY
P.O. Box 1037, Kansas City, Mo. 64140
Length of commitment: not specified.
Areas served: states of Wisconsin, Nebraska, Texas and New Mexico; Ethiopia and British Honduras.
Type of work done: teaching, nursing, social work with migrants and Indians; prison and inner-city work; work with youth and minority groups.

EXTENSION SOCIETY VOLUNTEERS
1307 South Wabash Ave., Chicago, Ill. 60605
Length of commitment: not specified.
Areas served: U.S.A.
Type of work done: teaching, nursing, coordination of Newman Centers and parish work.

JESUIT VOLUNTEERS CORPS
Length of commitment: in U.S.A., usually one school year; abroad, usually two years.
Areas served: Alaska, northwest U.S.A., Africa, British Honduras, Caroline Marshal Islands.
Type of work done: Jesuit volunteers are teachers, nurses, village workers, catechists, cooks, carpenters, radio technicians, construction workers, coaches, secretaries, librarians, youth workers. The biggest demands are for registered nurses and qualified teachers.

Other Organizations in the U.S.A.

PAPAL VOLUNTEERS FOR LATIN AMERICA
USCC, 1401 K Street, N.W., Washington, D.C. 20005

*ASSOCIATION FOR INTERNATIONAL DE-
VELOPMENT (AID)*
374 Grand Street, Paterson, N.J. 07505

INTERNATIONAL CATHOLIC AUXILIARIES
1734 Ashbury Ave., Evanston, Ill. 60204

REGIS COLLEGE LAY APOSTOLATE
Regis College, Weston, Mass. 02193

LAY COOPERATORS IN THE COMMUNICATIONS APOSTOLATE —THE PAULINE AUXILIARIES

Those who wish to help the timely apostolate of the media of social communication, may be interested in cooperating with the Daughters of St. Paul, a religious Congregation of pontifical right, established in thirty-one nations throughout the world. The Congregation's purpose is to spread the teachings of the Church in the spirit of the Gospel and Vatican II by means of the press, motion pictures, radio, television, filmstrips, records, tapes, cassettes, and any other means that human progress will provide in the years ahead.

Pauline Auxiliaries share the goals of the Daughters of St. Paul—their own sanctification and the salvation of many others.

The means of collaboration are three: prayer, activity, offerings.

Pauline Auxiliaries have their own manual of prayers, similar to that of members of the Congregation. Various daily and weekly practices are suggested in the manual. None of them oblige in conscience.

The most important apostolic activity an auxiliary could undertake would be the finding and encouraging of vocations to the Congregation. Auxiliaries may also cooperate by offering technical advice and help in the fields of printing, filmmaking, and recording. They may aid in the diffusion of wholesome Pauline editions by setting up parish libraries and pamphlet racks, making subscriptions, conducting book fairs or showing films.

Auxiliaries may also make or collect contributions to help the Congregation in its training of aspirants, postulants and novices and to enable it to purchase the equipment necessary to launch into new sectors of the communications apostolate.

Anyone wishing to receive further information on the Pauline Auxiliaries may write to or visit any of the St. Paul Catholic Book and Film Centers listed at the end of this book.

PRAYERS FOR THE COMMUNICATIONS APOSTOLATE

We praise and bless You, O Jesus, Divine Master, for having enlightened the mind of man to discover the new audiovisual techniques of the film, radio and television. Their mission is an apostolate: to educate and uplift men and society, materially and spiritually.

O almighty Father, You have created everything for us, as we are for Christ. May these inventions, too, sing Your glory as Creator and Savior.

Lead us not into temptation, O Lord, but deliver us from the evil of turning to ruin the gifts given to us by You with such wisdom and love.

Direct those responsible for these media to work with charity, and with respect for innocence and the dignity of man. May they always sow good seed, and be alert that the enemy may never sow weeds. Enlighten all listeners and viewers to seek the springs of living water and to shun the stagnant wells.

In reparation for every abuse, we offer You our daily work together with all the Masses that will be celebrated today throughout the world. We promise always to use the media of communication for our sanctification and for the apostolate.

O Jesus, Divine Master, through the intercession of Mary, Queen of the Apostles, and of St. Paul the Apostle, grant that through these media all men may come to know You as the Father has sent You: Way, Truth and Life. Amen.

Glory be to the Father.... (three times)

O Heavenly Father, I thank You for having chosen from among the angels, St. Gabriel to bring the announcement of the Incarnation and the redemption of mankind. Mary accepted the tidings with faith, and Your Son became incarnate and, by dying on the cross, redeemed all men.

But the majority of men have not yet received the message of salvation, and continue to live in darkness.

O St. Gabriel, patron of the communications media—film, radio and television—beseech Jesus Master, that as soon as possible the Church may use these powerful means to preach the divine truth to be believed, to show the way to be followed, to communicate the means of grace and of eternal happiness.

May these gifts of God serve in the uplifting and saving of all men.

May they never be used to spread error and ruin souls.

May everyone docilely accept the message of Jesus Christ.

O St. Gabriel, pray for us and for the communications apostolate. Amen.

FURTHER READING TO DEEPEN OUR FAITH

"Let the laity devotedly strive to acquire a more profound grasp of revealed truth...."
— DOGMATIC CONSTITUTION ON THE CHURCH

All of the following publications plus a complete booklist may be obtained from any of the addresses listed at the end of this book:

THE CATECHISM OF MODERN MAN
compiled by Daughters of St. Paul
The only complete sourcebook on the Council's new and profound expression of the Faith—all in the words of Vatican II and related post-conciliar documents. 9,000 topics.
731 pages; clothbound $5.95

THE CHRIST OF VATICAN II
compiled by Daughters of St. Paul
To a world that has in a sense lost a consciousness of things divine, and where a "death of God" theology is in vogue, the Second Vatican Council presents a vivid and vibrant profile of Christ the Lord.

The Christ of Vatican II is not a "new" Christ. He is the Sovereign, Master, Hero, Companion and Friend to whom the Scriptures bear witness, whom the Fathers and Doctors of the Church proclaimed over the centuries, and whom contemporary man sorely needs. 80 pages; Cloth $2

THE CHURCH IN OUR DAY
The Bishops of the United States
A collective pastoral letter on the life and development
of the American Catholic Church in the light of Vatican II.
"A truly magnificent document. I earnestly trust that all
our clergy, religious and laity will read and study it with
great care" (Most Rev. Bernard J. Flanagan, Bishop of
Worcester, Mass).

104 pages; Paper 60c; pamphlet 35c

THE CHURCH – LIGHT OF ALL MANKIND
Pope Paul VI
Ecumenism; the nature, marks, and missionary vocation
of the Church; the mission of the laity, the proper balance
between concern for the world and the necessary de-
tachment of the Christian whose goal is beyond this world;
devotion to the Holy Spirit and its relationship to respect
for the visible Church; the importance of austerity, morti-
fication and obedience to the vitality of the Church; these
and other matters of similar relevance are treated.

156 pages; Cloth $2; Paper $1

THE CREED OF A CATHOLIC
Rev. Wilfred Hurley, C.S.P.
Keen insights into the Apostles' Creed.

153 pages; Cloth $3; Paper $2

GENERAL MORAL THEOLOGY
Most Rev. Antonio Lanza and Most Rev. Pietro Palazzini
General Moral Theology should be of practical use and a
comfort not only to priests and seminarians, but also to
lawyers and medical doctors.

240 pages; Cloth $4

CHRIST, HOPE OF THE WORLD
Igino Giordani
"Christ walked with man, that man might walk with
God." With divine care and precision Christ revealed His
true identity to groping human minds. This book cannot
simply be read and set aside, for it influences every aspect
of the life we are living on our earthly journey back to
Christ.

Deluxe $10; Cloth $7; Paper $5

CHRIST THE ANSWER
Rev. Peter Sullivan
Appealingly-presented apologetics stressing the implication of the divinity of Christ for the modern world. "Valuable reading for the layman or the person involved in CCD work" (Rev. Anton Wambach).

272 pages; Cloth $4; Paper $3; Magister Paperback 95c

JESUS LORD
Compiled by Rev. Charles Dollen
Passages give ample testimony to the living faith of the early Christian Church in the divinity of Christ and what this implied in the everyday life of the Christian.

264 pages; Cloth $3; Paper $2

Papal Documents

POPE LEO XIII
Condition of Working Classes　25c
On the Study of Sacred Scripture　25c
Unity of the Church　25c

POPE PIUS XI
Atheistic Communism　25c
Christian Education of Youth　25c
Christian Marriage　25c
Motion Pictures　15c
Social Reconstruction　25c

POPE PIUS XII
Addresses to Cloistered Religious　$1.25
The Assumption of the Blessed Virgin Mary　15c
Function of the State in the Modern World　25c
Holy Virginity　25c
Humani Generis　15c
The Mystical Body of Christ　25c
On Motion Pictures, Radio and Television　25c
Promotion of Biblical Studies　25c
The Sacred Liturgy (*Mediator Dei*)　25c
Sponsa Christi　$1.00

POPE JOHN XXIII
Christmas Message   5c
From the Beginning of our Priesthood   25c
Grateful Memory   15c
Mater et Magistra   25c
Near the Chair of Peter   25c
Paenitentiam Agere   15c
Peace Message   5c
Peace on Earth   25c
To Women Religious   15c

POPE PAUL VI

Addresses to Seminaries and Vocations   20c
Apostolic Exhortation to All Bishops in Peace and Communion with the Apostolic See, on the Fifth Anniversary of the Close of the Second Vatican Council.   20c
Apostolic Letter to Cardinal Maurice Roy, President of the Council of the Laity and of the Pontifical Commission Justice and Peace, on the Occasion of the Eightieth Anniversary of the Encyclical *Rerum Novarum* ("The Coming Eightieth")   25c
Credo of the People of God   10c
The Development of Peoples   25c
Ecclesiam Suam   25c
Heights of Heroism in Life of Pius XII   5c
Message to Priests   6c
Month of May   15c
Mystery of Faith   25c
New Horizons for Women Religious   15c
Of Human Life   15c
Priestly Celibacy   25c
Priests Should Be in the World, Not of the World   10c
To All Religious   15c

Vatican II Documents

Constitution on the Sacred Liturgy   25c
Decree on the Media of Social Communication   15c
Dogmatic Constitution on the Church *(Lumen Gentium)* 50c
Decree on Ecumenism   25c
Decree on the Catholic Churches of the Eastern Rite   15c

Declaration on Christian Education (*Gravissimum Educationis*) 15c

Declaration on the Attitude of the Church to Non-Christian Religions 10c

Decree Concerning the Pastoral Office of Bishops in the Church (*Christus Dominus*) 30c

Decree on the Adaptation and Renewal of Religious Life (*Perfectae Caritatis*) 14c

Decree on Priestly Training (*Optatam Totius*) 15c

Decree on the Apostolate of the Laity (*Apostolicam Actuositatem*) 30c

Dogmatic Constitution on Divine Revelation 25c

Declaration on Religious Freedom (*Dignitatis Humanae*) 20c

Decree on the Ministry and Life of Priests 30c

Decree on the Mission Activity of the Church 30c

Pastoral Constitution on the Church in the Modern World (*Gaudium et Spes*) 65c

Documents Implementing Vatican II

Apostolic Constitution on Fast and Abstinence 10c

Apostolic Constitution on Indulgences 20c

Apostolic Constitution on New Roman Missal (*Missale Romanum*). *And:* Motu Proprio on Liturgical Year and New Universal Roman Calendar (*Paschalis Mysterii*) 20c

Apostolic Constitution on the Post-Council Jubilee 10c

Apostolic Exhortation on the Renewal of the Religious Life According to the Teaching of the Second Vatican Council. 25c

Apostolic Letter Determining Norms for Expediting Marriage Cases. 10c

Apostolic Letter *Ecclesiae Sanctae* 35c

Apostolic Letter on Mixed Marriages (*Matrimonia Mixta*). *And:* Statement of U.S. Bishops on the Implementation of the Apostolic Letter on Mixed Marriages 25c

Council Closing Speeches 30c

Directory on Ecumenism 15c

Instruction on Contemplative Life and on the Enclosure of Nuns 25c

Instruction on the Liturgy   25c

Instruction on Mixed Marriages   15c

Instruction on Music in the Liturgy   20c

Instruction on the Renewal of Religious Formation   25c

Instruction on Worship of the Eucharistic Mystery   25c

Motu Proprio *Sacram Liturgiam*   15c

Norms for Permanent Restoration of the Diaconate   15c

Pastoral Instruction for the Application of the Decree of the Second Vatican Ecumenical Council on the Means of Social Communication   50c

Second Instruction on the Liturgy   15c

Third Instruction of the Correct Application of the Constitution on the Sacred Liturgy.   15c

Toward the Meeting of Religions—Suggestions for Dialogue   35c

Index

Daughters of St. Paul

In Massachusetts
50 St. Paul's Avenue, *Boston*, Mass. 02130
172 Tremont Street, *Boston*, Mass. 02111
In New York
78 Fort Place, *Staten Island*, N.Y. 10301
625 East 187th Street, *Bronx*, N.Y. 10458
525 Main Street, *Buffalo*, N.Y. 14203
In Connecticut
202 Fairfield Avenue, *Bridgeport*, Conn. 06603
In Ohio
2105 Ontario St. (at Prospect Ave.), *Cleveland*, Ohio 44115
In Pennsylvania
1127 South Broad Street, *Philadelphia*, Pa. 19147
In Florida
2700 Biscayne Blvd., *Miami*, Florida 33137
In Louisiana
4403 Veterans Memorial Blvd., Metairie, *New Orleans*, La. 70002
86 Bolton Avenue, *Alexandria*, La. 71301
In Texas
114 East Main Plaza, *San Antonio*, Texas 78205
In California
1570 Fifth Avenue, *San Diego*, Calif. 92101
278 17th Street, *Oakland*, Calif. 94612
46 Geary Street, *San Francisco*, Calif. 94108
In Canada
3022 Dufferin Street, *Toronto* 395, Ontario, Canada
In England
57, Kensington Church Street, *London* W. 8, England
In Australia
58, Abbotsford Rd., Homebush, N.S.W., *Sydney* 2140, Australia
In Philippine Islands
2650, F.B. Harrison, P.O. Box 3576, *Pasay City*, Manila,
Philippine Islands
In India
143, Waterfield Road, Bandra, *Bombay*, 50-AS, India
In Africa
35, Jones Street, P.O. Box 3243, *Lagos*, Nigeria

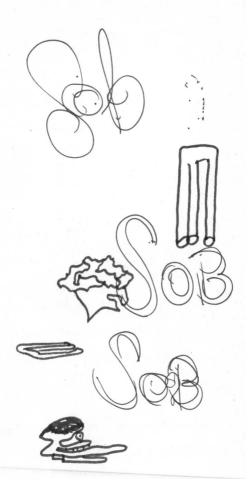